Christian
Handbook

Christian Handbook

A STRAIGHTFORWARD GUIDE TO THE BIBLE, CHURCH HISTORY & CHRISTIAN DOCTRINE

PETER JEFFERY

EVANGELICAL PRESS OF WALES

© Evangelical Press of Wales, 1988
First published 1988
ISBN 1 85049 044 9

Designed by Tony Cantale Graphics

Unless otherwise indicated, all Bible quotations are taken
from the New International Version.

Published by the **Evangelical Press of Wales**
Bryntirion, Bridgend, Mid Glamorgan, CF31 4DX
Printed by The Bath Press, Bath

Contents

Illustrations

Foreword

It is with great pleasure that I write a brief foreword to this very useful, informative and well-written book. It comes from the hand of one whom I am glad to count among my friends and brothers in the gospel ministry and who, under the rich blessing of God, has had powerful and fruitful ministries in the pastorates in which he has served.

Peter Jeffery is not just one of the most gifted preachers of our time, however. He is also a pastor of the people of God and is deeply concerned that Christian believers become strong, useful and godly. This concern was aroused by the very success which the Lord gave him in his ministry and deepened by the needs which he saw in many converts, and it led him to produce a series of books which have proved invaluable in helping many young Christians to attain maturity in the faith. This is his latest book, and it is well fitted to achieve the same aim.

The book is unusual in that it combines a brief survey of the Bible and its teaching with a short history of the church and an outline of the leading doctrines of the Christian faith. In attempting as much as this, the author set himself a daunting task, but he has accomplished it well. He has given us a work which will be useful not just to the new Christian convert, but to the student and scholar as well.

The information to be found here is always useful and is given in clear, understandable language. The author draws upon various writers of the best kind in each discipline. The frequent quotations from them serve two useful purposes: they illustrate the topic in hand, and they introduce the reader to well-known theologians and Christian authors in a way that will interest him in the original sources themselves.

One of the things which conversion to Christ (or even a fresh spiritual awakening in the life of a Christian) always does is to arouse interest in the Word of God, in what that Word has accomplished over the centuries, and in the great fundamental doctrines which the Bible teaches. This book caters for that interest in a way that no other book known to me manages to achieve.

Whoever you are, or wherever you are, when this book catches your attention, I advise you to acquire it. You will have in this book a work to which you can turn again and again and always find help, information and encouragement of the very best kind. I am grateful to my friend for the time and energy he has devoted to the preparation of this useful handbook for us. I pray that, with God's blessing, it will be greatly used and greatly blessed for many years to come.

J. DOUGLAS MACMILLAN
Free Church College, Edinburgh
September 1987

Introduction

When a person becomes a Christian, a glorious spiritual change takes place in his life. In addition to that, however, he is introduced to a whole new area of facts and knowledge which either he did not know about before or which he used to regard as uninteresting.

He starts to read the Bible. But what is the Bible? Who wrote it? Is it reliable? What does it contain?

He begins to attend church. But what is the church? How did it originate? Why is it so important to Christianity?

He wants to understand the teachings of Christianity. But who is Jesus? What is sin? What do justification, reconciliation and redemption mean?

If the new Christian is to grow in his faith, these questions must be grappled with and his understanding broadened. Good ministry and teaching in his church are the prime means by which this is accomplished. But the new believer also needs to study for himself. The aim of this handbook is to introduce him to all the basic facts that he needs to know — information which would otherwise only be available in much larger and more expensive volumes. I have therefore tried to be brief, simple and accurate.

Peter Jeffery

PART ONE
THE BIBLE

1
How the Bible was written

The Bible is unique. There is a vast amount of literature available in the world, but there is nothing quite like this remarkable book. It has been rightly said that while all books *in*form, and some may even *re*form, only one book *trans*forms. This is true because the Bible does not merely *contain* the Word of God; it *is* the Word of God. Consequently, it is essential for salvation: *'Faith cometh by hearing, and hearing by the word of God'* (Romans 10:17, AV). It is also essential for growth in the Christian faith: *'As newborn babes, desire the sincere milk of the word, that ye may grow thereby'* (1 Peter 2:2, AV).

There is no book so loved or so hated. Down through the centuries it has been banned in many countries, and it is still banned in some today. Yet men have been prepared to give their lives so that others may possess a Bible in their own language. The reason why it is so loved and hated is one and the same — because it is the Word of God. Men who love God will love His Word; men who oppose God will oppose His Word.

When we say that the Bible is the Word of God, we do not mean that God actually wrote it. He is its Author, but the Bible was written by men: *'Men spoke from God as they were carried along by the Holy Spirit'* (2 Peter 1:21). In other words, men were inspired by God to write. In this connection there are two words that it is important for us to understand: they are *inspiration* and *revelation*.

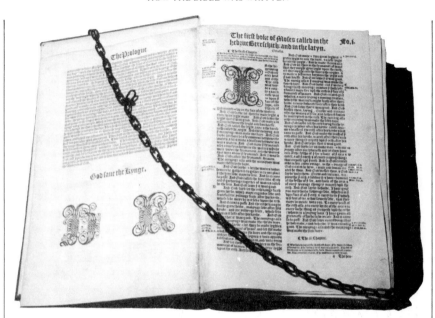

A chained copy of the Great Bible of 1539. It was called the Great Bible because of its size, which made it more suitable for use in the pulpit than in the home.

Inspiration

In 2 Timothy 3:16 the apostle Paul tells us that *'All scripture is given by inspiration of God'* (AV). The NIV translation says, *'All Scripture is God-breathed'* — and that is what it literally means. When we speak, our breath is in the words and it enables them to give expression to our thoughts. In the same way, the breath of God is in every word of Scripture. As the apostle Peter puts it, the Scripture *'never had its origin in the will of man, but men spoke from God as they were carried along by the Holy Spirit'* (2 Peter 1:21).

Inspiration means that the human writers who actually wrote the books of the Bible were guided and directed by God the Holy Spirit. This does not mean that God dictated everything to them word for word. Inspiration is not mechanical. Moses, Paul and the other writers were not merely secretaries taking down dictation, but they were men 'carried along by the Holy Spirit'. God so directed their thinking and their understanding that the message they gave was not their own invention, but a faithful expression of the mind of God. *'This is what we speak, not in words taught us by human wisdom but in words taught by the Spirit, expressing spiritual truths in spiritual words'* (1 Corinthians 2:13).

While every word of the Bible is God-breathed, it is expressed through different men with

A surviving example of Miles Coverdale's Bible of 1535. This was the first complete printed Bible in English.

different styles and thought-forms. The Holy Spirit did not suppress the personality of the writers but used it. As William Hendriksen wrote:

❝ *We find in Scripture a wide variety of style and language. There is a vast difference between the deeply emotional tenor of Hosea and the vividly descriptive manner of expression which characterizes Nahum; between the exhortations of Haggai and Hebrews, and the argumentations of Malachi and Galatians. Nevertheless, all are equally the Word of God.* ❞

Sometimes, to describe what they mean by inspiration,

Christians use two technical words — *plenary* and *verbal*. Plenary inspiration means that the *entire* Bible is God-given — and this includes its historical sections as well as its doctrinal teachings. Verbal inspiration means that the actual *words* used in the Bible are God-given.

Revelation

The second important word for us to understand is the word *revelation*. Dr J.I. Packer explains it like this:

❝ *'Reveal' is a picture-word (as, indeed, all theological words are), and the picture is of 'God unveiling' - God showing us things which were previously hidden from us, God bringing into the open things which before were out of our sight, God causing and enabling us to see what hitherto we could not see. God takes us into his confidence and shares his secrets with us; God finds us ignorant, and gives us knowledge. That is what revelation means.* 🙶

If God had not chosen to reveal Himself to us, we would never know anything about Him. God's revelation takes two forms — *general* and *special. General revelation* is described by the psalmist: *'The heavens declare the glory of God; the skies proclaim the work of his hands'* (Psalm 19:1). This revelation is so clear that it leaves man 'without excuse'

St Catherine's Monastery at the foot of Jebel Musa, the mountain which many believe is the biblical Mount Sinai. It was at this monastery that the earliest complete manuscript of the New Testament, the Codex Sinaiticus, was discovered.

if he ignores it (Romans 1:20). But sin has so blinded man's heart and mind that general revelation will never lead him to God and to salvation. For this, there must be *special revelation.* The Bible is the record of God's special revelation to man. It records what God has done and said concerning our salvation. It is God's revealed truth.

The purpose of this revelation is not only to tell us about God but, above all, to bring us by faith to know God. It is God reaching down into man's hopelessness with the supreme revelation of Himself in the Person of the Lord Jesus Christ. Thus, it is a final revelation. God has no more to say to us. All we need in order to know God as Lord and Saviour has been revealed in Scripture. So we must reject all claims to new revelation bringing us doctrines

contrary to those taught in the Bible.

John Robinson, who was the pastor of the Pilgrim Fathers, was right when he said that the Lord had *'more truth and light yet to break forth out of His holy Word'*. We must never close our minds to the Holy Spirit speaking to us and teaching us from the Bible things we never properly understood. But that is not the same as new revelation. To discover new truths *in* the Scriptures is a thrilling experience; but to *add* so-called new truths *to* the Scriptures is fatal.

If the Bible is the inspired Word of God and the special revelation to man of the mind and will of God, then it follows inevitably that the Bible must be inerrant and the Christian's sole authority.

Inerrant

E.J. Young explains the word 'inerrant' in this way:

❝ *By this word we mean that the Scriptures possess the quality of freedom from error. They are exempt from the liability of mistake, incapable of error. In all their teachings they are in perfect accord with the truth.* **❞**

A Bible that was not inerrant or infallible would not be much use to us. If it is inspired, it must be infallible. Since God Himself is infallible, His Word must be infallible. Jesus confirmed this for us by the way He used Scripture. He said, for instance, *'the Scripture cannot be broken'* (John

This hexagonal clay prism (dating from the year 686 BC) gives an account of eight military campaigns conducted by Sennacherib (705-681 BC), king of Assyria. It records his invasion of Israel in 701 BC and tells how his army besieged Hezekiah in Jerusalem and received tribute from him (as described in 2 Kings 18:13-16).

10:35), and He showed His personal reliance upon it by continually quoting it in a variety of situations. For example, he used Scripture:

☐ to deal with Satan (Matthew 4:1-11),
☐ to deal with a seeking soul (Matthew 19:16-22),
☐ to deal with His enemies (Matthew 15:1-9),
☐ to explain the cross (John 3:14; Matthew 26:31).

Jesus Christ clearly believed in the existence of Adam and Eve (Matthew 19:4-5) and of Noah and the ark (Luke 17:26-27). He also believed that Jonah was swallowed by a large fish (Matthew 12:40).

It is often argued that there are many errors and contradictions in the Bible. We would readily agree that there are difficulties, but difficulties are not the same as errors. If you wish to give time to studying this subject, read Brian Edwards's book *Nothing But The Truth,* especially the last two chapters. Here is one quotation from that book:

" *There are two things we must never forget. In the first place, our belief in an errorless Bible is not based upon the fact that it can all be proved to be true; on the contrary we believe it because of its own claim . . . The second fact that we must not forget is that as scholars discover more and more about Bible language and Bible archaeology almost all their information shows the Bible to be accurate.* **"**

Authority

If the Bible is inspired and inerrant, then it must inevitably be the Christian's sole authority for what he believes and how he is to live. The Christian's great concern must be to please God and to live for the glory of God. The Bible tells us how to do this, for in this book *God* speaks to us. In the Old Testament, the words 'the Lord said', 'the Lord spoke' and 'the word of the Lord came' are used 3,808 times. God is speaking, and we are to listen and obey.

Biblical authority means that all teaching must be tested by what the Scriptures say. This is why it is so important for the Christian to know his Bible.

If the Bible is not our authority, then something else will be, and in all probability it will be our own

" *Arm yourself with a thorough knowledge of the written Word of God. Read your Bible . . . Neglect your Bible and nothing that I know of can prevent you from error if a plausible advocate of false teaching shall happen to meet you. Make it a rule to believe nothing except it can be proved from Scripture. The Bible alone is infallible.* **"**

J.C. Ryle

human understanding. The choice then is between what I think and what God has said. To make our own opinions our authority is really a most flimsy foundation on which to build.

66 *The church is built upon the foundation of the apostles and prophets. We must therefore reject every supposed new revelation, every addition to doctrine. We must assert that all teaching and all truth and all doctrine must be tested in the light of the Scriptures. Here is God's revelation of Himself, given in parts and portions in the Old Testament with an increasing clarity and with a culminating finality, coming*

*eventually 'in the fulness of times'
to the perfect, absolute, final
revelation in God the Son. He in
turn enlightens and reveals His will
and teaching to these apostles,
endows them with a unique
authority, fills them with the
needed ability and power, and
gives them the teaching that is
essential to the well-being of the*

Codex Sinaiticus, the earliest complete
copy of the New Testament in
existence. It dates from the 4th century
AD and is written in Greek. It is open at
Luke 19:30-20:34.

*church and God's people. We can
build only upon this one, unique,
authority.* **""**
D.M. Lloyd-Jones

2
How the Bible was compiled

The word 'Bible' comes from the Greek word *biblia,* meaning 'books'. The Bible is a collection of sixty-six books. Thirty-nine of them, which we call the Old Testament, were written originally in Hebrew (with a few short passages in Aramaic). The other twenty-seven, which are known as the New Testament, were written in Greek. These books were written by about forty men over a period of 1,500 years.

Clearly, the original manuscripts would not last for ever, and so they had to be copied. The men who copied them were called scribes. Our English Bible was translated from a copy of a copy of a copy . . . so how authentic is it? We find it hard to imagine these manuscripts being copied out by hand without any mistakes. Undoubtedly some mistakes were made, but the scribes were amazingly meticulous in checking and correcting their work.

66 *After the scribe finished copying a particular book, he would count all of the words and letters it contained. Then he checked this tally against the count for the manuscript that he was copying. He counted the number of times a particular word occurred in the book, and he noted the middle word and the middle letter in the book, comparing all of these with his original. By making these careful checks, he hoped to avoid any scribal errors.* **99**
Marshalls Bible Handbook

We can say then that these early scribes took great care to ensure that their copying was accurate, even counting every letter of every book to check that not one had been left out. As a matter of fact, the Hebrew word for 'scribe' originally meant 'to count'.

During the 1,500 years that the Bible was being written, many other books were written for which some sort of authority was claimed. In the Old Testament era, for instance, there were the books of the Apocrypha, and in the New Testament era there were writings such as *The Shepherd of Hermas* and *The Epistle of Barnabas.* Why are these not included in our Bible? And how were those sixty-six books chosen for inclusion in what we regard as the inspired Scriptures?

The collection of books that makes up our Bible is known as the *canon* of Scripture. This is a Greek word meaning the 'rule' or 'standard' by which something is measured, and the term means that the Bible itself is our rule, our standard, our authority. It was not that a group of men decided on a standard by which to judge which books should be included in the Bible, but rather that these sixty-six books clearly carried divine authority and were marked out as different from all other books. The church did not *give* Scripture its authority; it merely recognized and acknowledged the authority that it had.

The Old Testament

There is an old Jewish tradition that it was Ezra who first compiled the Old Testament canon, even though there were collections of the first five books (known as the Pentateuch) and some of the prophets long before his time. We can never be sure how these thirty-nine books were put together, but we know that by the time Jesus was born the books of the Old Testament had been agreed upon.

The books of the Jewish Old Testament were divided into three groups — the Law, the Prophets and the Writings. *The Law* consisted of the five books written by Moses: Genesis, Exodus, Leviticus, Numbers and Deuteronomy. *The Prophets* included Joshua, Judges, Samuel, Kings, Isaiah, Jeremiah, Ezekiel, and also the prophets from Hosea to Malachi in our Bible today. *The Writings* were Psalms, Proverbs, Job, Song of Solomon, Ruth, Lamentations, Ecclesiastes, Esther, Daniel, Ezra, Nehemiah and Chronicles.

The order of the books in our English Bible is that of the Septuagint, a Greek translation of the Old Testament made in the second century BC. The Bible that Jesus used and so often referred to is our Old Testament, and most of its thirty-nine books are quoted in the New Testament.

The New Testament

Most of the twenty-seven New Testament books were written within forty years of the death of Jesus, and all of them within seventy years, but it was not until AD 397 that the canon was finally agreed.

It is clear from the New Testament itself that the early church regarded the thirty-nine Old Testament books as the Word of God. They are repeatedly quoted in the New Testament as authoritative. But to give complete expression to the Christian faith, more than this was needed. At first, of course, the apostles would be able to give a spoken testimony to the truth; but after their death a written record was required. So God in His goodness gave the church the New Testament. By the close of the second century, the four Gospels (Matthew, Mark, Luke and John), together with the book of Acts, were commonly regarded as the early authentic history of Christ and His church. There is little doubt that by this

THE CONTENTS OF THE BIBLE

LAW & HISTORY

Genesis
Exodus
Leviticus
Numbers
Deuteronomy

HISTORY

Joshua
Judges
Ruth
1 Samuel
2 Samuel
1 Kings
2 Kings
1 Chronicles
2 Chronicles
Ezra
Nehemiah
Esther

WISDOM & POETRY

Job
Psalms
Proverbs
Ecclesiastes
Song of Solomon

PROPHECY

Isaiah
Jeremiah
Lamentations
Ezekiel
Daniel
Hosea
Joel
Amos
Obadiah
Jonah
Micah
Nahum
Habakkuk
Zephaniah
Haggai
Zechariah
Malachi

OLD TESTAMENT

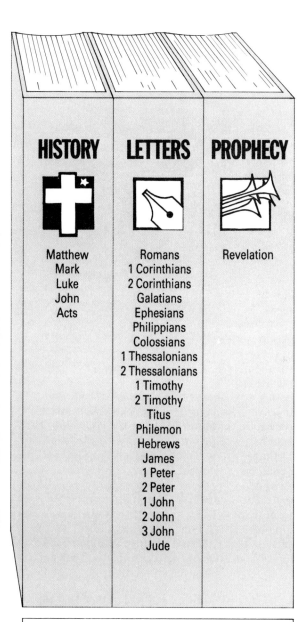

HISTORY

Matthew
Mark
Luke
John
Acts

LETTERS

Romans
1 Corinthians
2 Corinthians
Galatians
Ephesians
Philippians
Colossians
1 Thessalonians
2 Thessalonians
1 Timothy
2 Timothy
Titus
Philemon
Hebrews
James
1 Peter
2 Peter
1 John
2 John
3 John
Jude

PROPHECY

Revelation

N E W   T E S T A M E N T

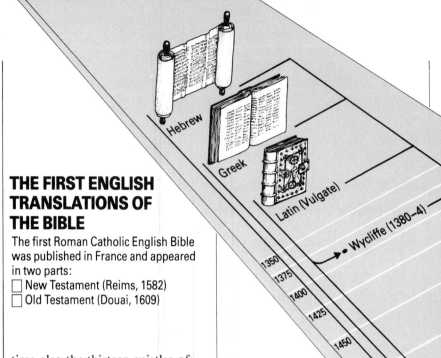

Hebrew

Greek

Latin (Vulgate)

Wycliffe (1380-4)

1350
1375
1400
1425
1450
1475
1500

THE FIRST ENGLISH TRANSLATIONS OF THE BIBLE

The first Roman Catholic English Bible was published in France and appeared in two parts:

☐ New Testament (Reims, 1582)
☐ Old Testament (Douai, 1609)

time also the thirteen epistles of Paul were accepted as inspired. In fact, most of the twenty-seven New Testament books were generally accepted by Christians; but there was hesitation over a few of them including James, Jude and 2 Peter. Besides this, many other books were circulating among the churches. The situation needed clarification, and so the churches of the West gathered at Carthage in AD 397 and settled the content of the New Testament once and for all. Two tests were applied to the many books in circulation. Did the book come from the time of the apostles? And did its teaching agree with known apostolic doctrine?

❝ *It is clear that the New Testament canon was not the result of ecclesiastical pronouncements, but grew in accordance with the* *needs of the church. The major factor governing selection was 'apostolicity' — the conviction that the books represented the position of the apostolic age.* **❞**
Donald Guthrie

English Translations

To have an Old Testament in Hebrew and a New Testament in Greek would not be much use to us. We need a Bible in English so that we can read the Word of God for ourselves. Amazingly, it was not until the early 1380s that the first complete English Bible appeared, translated from the Latin Bible by John Wycliffe and his followers. Even then it was not welcomed by the official Roman Catholic Church, which condemned Wycliffe and burnt many of the handwritten copies of his Bible.

William Tyndale, the next great translator into English, faced similar opposition from the Roman Catholic Church. In 1525 he completed his translation of the New Testament; it was printed in Germany, and copies were smuggled into England. In 1536 Tyndale was burnt at the stake for daring to translate the Scriptures into the language of the common man.

Two years later, King Henry VIII ordered that an English translation of the Bible should be placed in every parish church in his kingdom. It became known as the

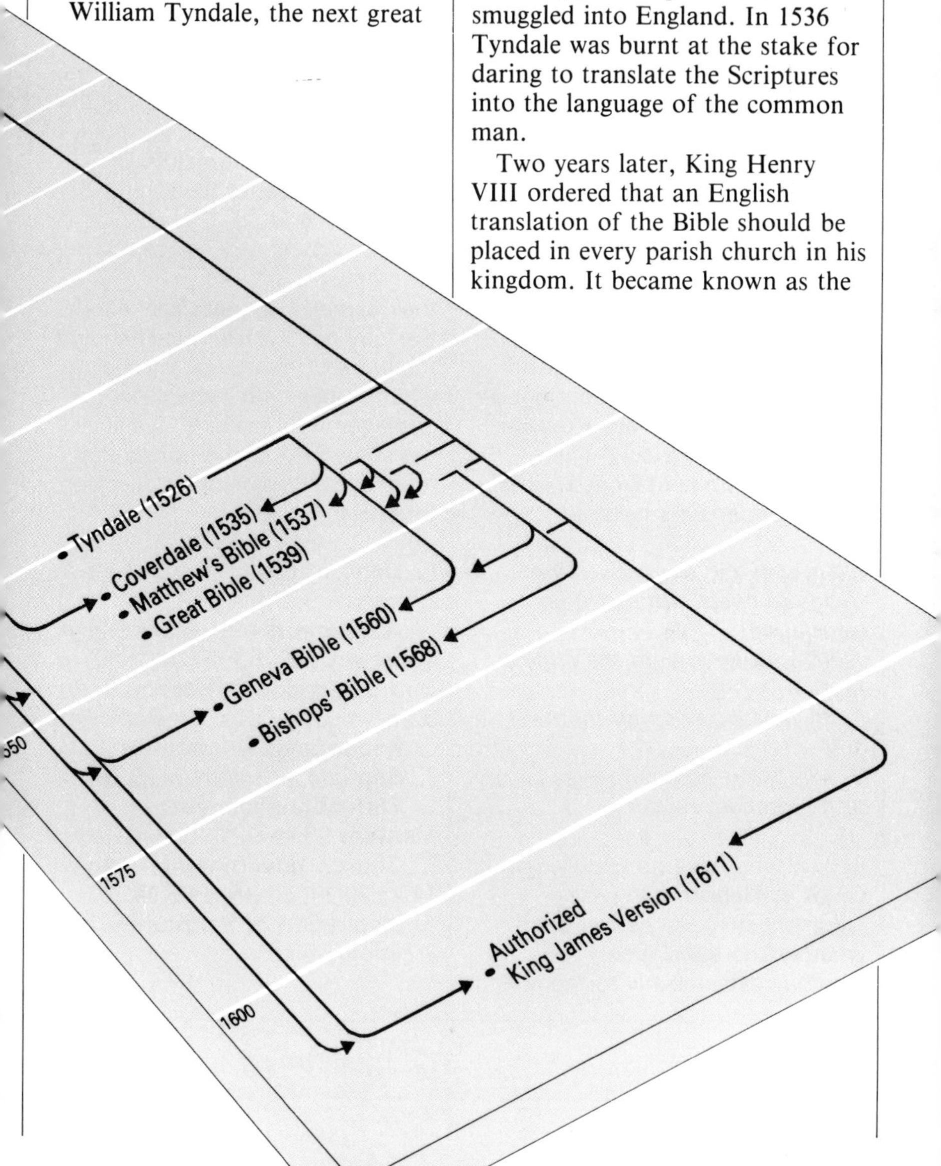

Tyndale (1526)
Coverdale (1535)
Matthew's Bible (1537)
Great Bible (1539)
Geneva Bible (1560)
Bishops' Bible (1568)
Authorized King James Version (1611)

1550
1575
1600

'Great Bible' because of its size. The Great Bible was Miles Coverdale's revision of earlier translations by Tyndale and himself. Then in 1553 Mary Tudor became queen; she was an ardent Roman Catholic, and again all English Bibles were banned.

The next major translation of the Bible into English became known as the Geneva Bible and was first printed in 1560. It was therefore in use during the reign of Queen Elizabeth I (1558-1603), and it was the first edition of the Bible to divide the text into verses.

James I became king in 1603, and the following year he appointed fifty-four scholars to make a new translation of the Bible. This was first published in 1611, and it became known as the King James Version or the Authorized Version. Without doubt, until recent years at least, this is the version which has reigned supreme in the English-speaking world.

Testing Translations

Today, there are many English translations available, some good and some not so good. How can we tell which is which? The following comment from *Marshalls Bible Handbook* is helpful:

❝ In general, there are three things to check out in a Bible translation:
1. its attitude toward the original text,
2. its way of rendering that text, and
3. whether it communicates clearly to the modern reader. ❞

People who have no knowledge of Greek or Hebrew can pass judgment only on the last point — whether the translation communicates clearly to them. But they can learn a great deal about the way each version has handled the work of translation by seeing what it does with certain key passages. For example, we shall get some idea of the translators' theological viewpoint by checking these references:

☐ **Deity of Christ** — John 1:1; Romans 9:5; Titus 2:13
☐ **Atonement** — Romans 3:25; Hebrews 2:17; 1 John 2:2;4:10
☐ **Justification** — Romans 3:25; 5:1
☐ **Repentance** — Matthew 3:2
☐ **Baptism** — Matthew 28:19
☐ **Eternal punishment** — Matthew 25:46
☐ **Church government** — Acts 14:23;20:17,28; James 5:14
☐ **Inspiration of Scripture** — 2 Timothy 3:16

3
The Old Testament

It is impossible to give accurate dates to the events recorded in the Old Testament, particularly those before the time of Abraham. But we do know that the period extending from Abraham to the time of Christ was about 2,000 years. In order to gain some understanding of the overall content of the Old Testament, we must break it down into digestible sections.

Before we do this, however, it is important for us to understand the purpose of the Old Testament. It is dismissed by some as nothing more than a series of bloodthirsty battles between warring tribes, and the actions of an angry God towards a small nation, Israel. The Old Testament, these people would say, has nothing to do with Christianity. Such opinions are to be totally rejected.

66 There is one, central theme which, like a golden thread, runs through all the stories of the Old Testament. That theme is The Coming Christ. *As long as one does not see this, the Old Testament remains a* closed *book. As soon as this idea is grasped, the Scriptures are* opened. *99*
William Hendriksen

Such a view agrees perfectly with the New Testament and the teaching of Jesus. The Saviour chose to explain His death and resurrection to two bewildered disciples by quoting the Old Testament to them: *'And beginning with Moses and all the Prophets, he explained to them what was said in all the Scriptures concerning himself'* (Luke 24:27). When dealing with Jewish leaders in Rome, the apostle Paul followed his Master's example: *'From morning till evening he explained and declared to them the kingdom of God and tried to convince them about Jesus from the Law of Moses and from the Prophets'* (Acts 28:23). If, therefore, we are to have a full appreciation of biblical Christianity, we must have an understanding of the Old Testament.

It is customary now for the thirty-nine Old Testament books to

Dead Sea salt pillar.

be divided into four sections, as follows:

☐ **The Law** — Genesis, Exodus, Leviticus, Numbers and Deuteronomy. (This section is also called 'The Pentateuch'.)
☐ **History** — Joshua, Judges, Ruth, Samuel, Kings, Chronicles, Ezra, Nehemiah, Esther.
☐ **Poetry** — Job, Psalms, Proverbs, Ecclesiastes, Song of Solomon.
☐ **Prophets** — Isaiah, Jeremiah, Lamentations, Ezekiel, Daniel, Hosea, Joel, Amos, Obadiah, Jonah, Micah, Nahum, Habakkuk, Zephaniah, Haggai, Zechariah, Malachi.

This helps us to see where the thirty-nine books fit in, but it does not tell us much about their content. For this we shall break it down in a different way, by tracing first the Old Testament story.

The Patriarchs

From the creation to the time of Joseph we see God dealing with certain outstanding men whom we call 'the patriarchs'. In this period we have momentous events such as the fall of man into sin and the entrance of death as the inevitable consequence of sin. God's anger against sin is vividly demonstrated in the flood; yet, amidst the awfulness of that judgment, we see one man responding in faith to God: *'By faith Noah . . .'* (Hebrews 11:7).

About the year 2,000 BC God spoke to Abraham. This was an event of great spiritual significance. The patriarch Abraham is described in the New Testament as *'the father of all who believe'* (Romans 4:11).

❝ *His life is an illustration of the manner in which men, in all ages, are saved (Romans 4:3). God's covenant with him (Genesis 17) is still in force. Scripture clearly teaches that it was never abrogated (Galatians 3:17). It applies to all believers: 'And if ye are Christ's, then are ye Abraham's seed, heirs according to promise' (Galatians 3:29).* **❞**
William Hendriksen

The stories of Isaac, Jacob and Joseph reveal God's providential hand and sovereign grace in dealing with men.

Moses and the Promised Land

God's providence and sovereignty are also clearly seen in the life of Moses. He is chosen, prepared, and used in a most remarkable way. The Passover, the Exodus and the Ten Commandments all demonstrate God's goodness in providing for His people, and the forty years in the wilderness show that the Holy One will not tolerate sin in His redeemed. It was during this period that

❝ *. . . sacrifice was ordained as the visible means whereby the guilty might find pardon. It was a powerful reminder that the wages of sin is death, and that without*

the shedding of blood is no remission. ""
G.T. Manley

This does not mean that no sacrifices were offered before the time of Moses. We find Abel and Noah sacrificing to God. But the Mosaic ritual was the specific command of God and therefore obligatory for all men.

Ultimately, despite every obstacle raised both by God's people and by their enemies, the Promised Land is reached. Still the people sin and God punishes them. When they cry to Him in repentance, He sends judges to save them.

The Kings

During the time of Samuel, who was the last of the judges, the people demanded a king to rule over them. In asking for this, they were in effect rejecting the unique relationship which existed between them and God (1 Samuel 8:7). The kingship of Almighty God was to be replaced by the kingship of a mere man. God warned them through Samuel of the consequences (1 Samuel 8:10-18). The people, however, refused to listen. *'No!'*, they said, *'We want a king over us. Then we shall be like all other nations'* (verses 19-20).

God gave them what they wanted, and Saul became the first king, to be followed by David and Solomon. In both Saul and David we see early blessing and success followed by terrible sin. Saul's sin leads to embitterment and

rebellion, and ultimately to his rejection by God. David's sin leads to genuine sorrow and repentance, and to God's forgiveness; but the consequences of his sin still have to be faced. Solomon's reign starts in true magnificence and continues in this way for many years, but his many foreign wives lead him astray (1 Kings 11:1-6). The full effects of this are not apparent until after his death.

Two Kingdoms

Solomon died in 931 BC and was

Great Sea (Mediterranean Sea)

Memphis●

EGYPT

THE ANCIENT NEAR EAST AT THE TIME OF THE PATRIARCHS

R. Nile

succeeded by his son Rehoboam. This foolish man alienated the already disgruntled northern tribes (1 Kings 12), and his kingdom collapsed as a result. As the king of Judah, he continued to rule from Jerusalem over two tribes (Judah and Benjamin), while Jeroboam ruled in the north over the other ten tribes as the king of Israel. Thus the people of God were divided and at war with each other. This tragic situation continued for 350 years, until finally God brought the whole sad story to an end. In 586 BC He allowed Nebuchadnezzar, king of Babylon, to destroy the southern kingdom. The northern kingdom had already fallen to Assyria in 722 BC, so now both kingdoms had come to an end and very many of the people were in exile in foreign lands.

The Exile

Jeremiah had prophesied that the Babylonian exile would last for seventy years (Jeremiah 25:11). This was God's judgment upon

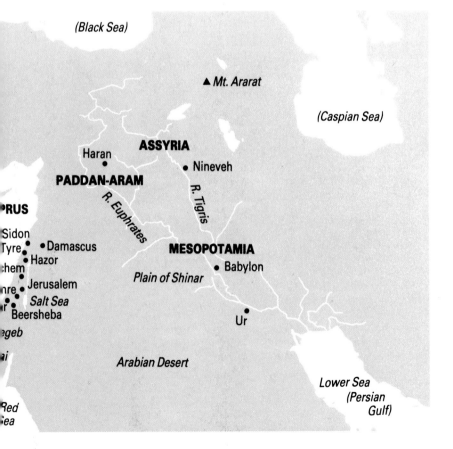

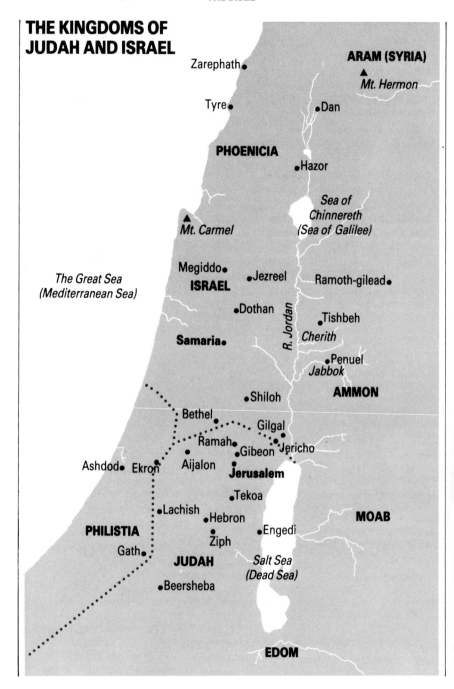

THE KINGDOMS OF JUDAH AND ISRAEL

Zarephath

ARAM (SYRIA)

▲ Mt. Hermon

Tyre

Dan

PHOENICIA

Hazor

Sea of Chinnereth (Sea of Galilee)

▲ Mt. Carmel

Megiddo

ISRAEL

Jezreel

Ramoth-gilead

The Great Sea (Mediterranean Sea)

Dothan

R. Jordan

Tishbeh

Cherith

Samaria

Penuel

Jabbok

AMMON

Shiloh

Bethel

Gilgal

Ramah

Gibeon

Jericho

Ashdod

Ekron

Aijalon

Jerusalem

Tekoa

Lachish

Hebron

Engedi

MOAB

PHILISTIA

Ziph

Gath

JUDAH

Salt Sea (Dead Sea)

Beersheba

EDOM

them. But it was more than that, for during the exile God was going to refine these people in the crucible of suffering. His purpose was to create in them a new heart, so that He could bring them back to their own land to serve Him as they ought (Jeremiah 24:5-7). The prophet Ezekiel, who was sent by God to minister to the exiles, foretold that a remnant would return to Jerusalem.

The Return

Just as God had used a pagan king, Nebuchadnezzar, to take His people into exile, so also He used a pagan king to bring them out of exile. Babylon was conquered by Cyrus, king of Persia, and in 538 BC he allowed the exiles to return to their own land. His decree about this is recorded for us in Ezra 1:2-4. On their return, the exiles found Jerusalem in a state of utter desolation, but they were encouraged by the prophets Haggai and Zechariah to rebuild. Ezra and Nehemiah also played important parts in rebuilding the city and re-establishing the law of God.

The Old Testament closes in about 400 BC with God's reminder to His people through the prophet Malachi that they are His treasured possession, and His promise that *'for you who revere my name, the sun of righteousness will rise with healing in its wings'* (Malachi 4:2).

The Cylinder of Cyrus, king of Babylonia from 539-530 BC. The cylinder dates from 536 BC and records how Cyrus captured Babylon and allowed those who lived in exile there to return to their own lands. These exiled peoples included the Jews (see Ezra 1).

A religious Jew near the Western Wall in Jerusalem. This is the site of Herod's temple, which was destroyed by the Romans in AD 70. The man is receiving help to put on a phylactery.
A phylactery is a black leather box containing four Scripture passages: Exodus 13:1-10 and 13:11-16; Deuteronomy 6:4-9 and 11:13-21. One phylactery is strapped to the forehead and another to the left arm with the aid of thongs.

—— Old Testament Worship ——

Sacrifices

The sacrificial system in the Old Testament highlights two basic biblical truths, namely, the holiness of God and the sinfulness of man. If man is to approach God, he must come in a way that is acceptable to Him, and that means that atonement must be made for his sin (Leviticus 1:3-4). The importance of this is seen in the account of Cain and Abel approaching God (Genesis 4). Why is it that Abel is accepted and Cain rejected? The answer is in verses 3-4: *'The Lord looked with favour on Abel and his offering, but on Cain and his offering he did not look with favour'*. The key to their acceptance or rejection was the offering that each brought.

God did not leave man to work

out what He required. He gave Israel a detailed system, showing how they could approach Him with the assurance of being accepted. In the book of Leviticus five types of sacrifice are prescribed: the burnt offering, grain offering, peace offering, sin offering and guilt offering.

" *When the offender's sins have been removed (symbolized by the sin offering) and his life has been wholly consecrated to Jehovah (indicated by the burnt offering), nothing now prevents him from exercising blessed fellowship with his God (pictured by the peace offering): cf. Romans 5:1.* **"**
William Hendriksen

Festivals
Essential for the worshipper in the Old Testament were the four great festivals:

□ **The Passover,** or **The Feast of Unleavened Bread**
This began on the evening of the fourteenth day of the first month (Abib). It celebrated the Passover and the release from bondage in Egypt (Exodus 12; Deuteronomy 16).

" *The ceremony was full of symbolism. The blood of the animal symbolized the cleansing of sins. Bitter herbs represented the bitterness of bondage in Egypt. And the unleavened bread was a symbol of purity.* **"**
Marshalls Bible Handbook

□ **The Feast of Weeks (Pentecost)**
This feast was held fifty days after the Feast of Unleavened Bread. It marked the end of the harvest (Leviticus 23:15-22).

The —Old Testament— Calendar

Months	No.	Name
April	1	Nisan (Abib)
May	2	Iyyar (Ziv)
June	3	Sivan
July	4	Tammuz
August	5	Ab
September	6	Elul
October	7	Tishri (Ethanim)
November	8	Marchesvan (Bul)
December	9	Kislev
January	10	Tebeth
February	11	Shebat
March	12	Adar

—— Kings and Prophets ——

Date	Judah	Israel	
931 BC	Rehoboam	Jeroboam	
	Abijah	Nadab	
	Asa	Baasha	
900			
	Jehoshaphat	Elah	
		Zimri	
		Tibni	
		Omri	
		Ahab	Elijah
850			
	Jehoram		
	Ahaziah	Ahaziah	
		Joram	
	Athaliah	Jehu	
	Joash (Jehoash)	Jehoahaz	
800			
	Amaziah	Joash	?Jonah
	Uzziah	Jeroboam II	
		Zechariah	
			Amos
		Shallum	
		Menahem	

☐ The Feast of Tabernacles

This feast commemorated Israel's wanderings in the wilderness (Leviticus 23:33-44), and began on the fifteenth day of the seventh month (Tishri).

☐ The Day of Atonement

This was Israel's most solemn holy day, the day for the cleansing of sins, when no work could be done and a strict fast had to be observed by all the people (Leviticus 16; 23:26-32). It took place on the tenth day of Tishri, just before the Feast of Tabernacles.

These Old Testament sacrifices and festivals are no longer to be observed, but what they represented and symbolized is the very essence of New Testament Christianity. The Epistle to the Hebrews makes this quite clear.

◄
A table prepared for the celebration of the Passover.

Date	Judah		Israel	
750				
			Pekahiah	
	Jotham		Pekah	Hosea
	Ahaz	Isaiah	Hoshea	
	Hezekiah	Micah	(722: Exile)	
700				
	Manasseh			
	Amon	Nahum		
	Josiah			
	Jehoahaz	Zephaniah		
		Habakkuk		
		Jeremiah		
	Jehoiakim			
600				
	Jehoiachin			
	Zedekiah			
	(586: Exile)			
		Obadiah		
		Daniel		
		Ezekiel		
	(538:Exile ends)			
		Haggai		
		Zechariah		
500				
		?Joel		
		Malachi		

4
The New Testament

For the purpose of this brief study of the New Testament we will divide the twenty-seven books into two sections. The first, which we shall call the *historical* section, is made up of the four Gospels and the book of Acts. Here we have actual eyewitness accounts of the events surrounding the lives of Jesus and His apostles (Luke 1:1-4). Almost all we know of the life of Jesus is recorded in the Gospels, and so these books are of the utmost importance to the Christian. After Acts, the remaining twenty-two books from Romans to Revelation can be described as the *doctrinal* (or teaching) section. Here we find the apostles instructing, exhorting and rebuking the church. What these books have to tell us is crucial for our understanding of the Christian faith and for Christian living.

—— History ——

The Gospels

Although these four books present us with a historical account of the life of Jesus, we must add that their authors did not set out to write orderly, detailed biographies. Their purpose was rather to show us Jesus Christ, the Son of God and the Saviour of the world, who came from heaven to die as an atonement for our sin. This being the case, the order in which events are recorded may differ from one Gospel to another, and different details may be presented. To obtain the full picture, therefore, we need to put the four Gospels together.

Matthew

This book was written primarily for the Jews, a people who knew the Old Testament well. Hence we find Matthew quoting frequently from the Old Testament in order to persuade them that Jesus was the Messiah of whom their own Scriptures had prophesied. (There are fifty-three Old Testament quotations in Matthew, as compared with thirty-six in Mark, twenty-five in Luke and twenty in

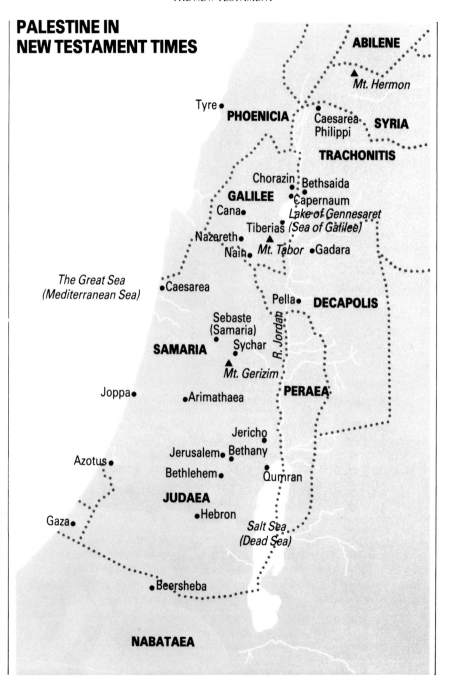

PALESTINE IN NEW TESTAMENT TIMES

ABILENE

▲ *Mt. Hermon*

Tyre •

PHOENICIA

• Caesarea
Philippi · **SYRIA**

TRACHONITIS

Chorazin • Bethsaida

GALILEE • Capernaum

Cana • *Lake of Gennesaret*

Tiberias *(Sea of Galilee)*

Nazareth •

Nain • *Mt. Tabor* • Gadara

*The Great Sea
(Mediterranean Sea)*

• Caesarea

Pella • **DECAPOLIS**

Sebaste
(Samaria)

SAMARIA • Sychar

▲
Mt. Gerizim

R. Jordan

PERAEA

Joppa •

• Arimathaea

Jericho
•

Jerusalem • Bethany

Azotus •

Bethlehem • Qumran

JUDAEA

• Hebron

Gaza •

*Salt Sea
(Dead Sea)*

• Beersheba

NABATAEA

Bethlehem with the bell tower of the
Church of the Nativity in the foreground.

> **“** *Each of the Gospel writers presents Jesus to us in his own characteristic way. The greatness of this person could not have been captured in one picture. So we have four portraits, each bringing out its own distinctive facets of the character of Jesus.* **”**
> The Lion Handbook to the Bible

John.) The opening verse of Matthew's Gospel indicates the book's particular emphasis:

“ *This verse gives us a clue to the special drift of Matthew's Gospel. He was moved of the Holy Spirit to write of our Lord Jesus as King — 'the son of David'.* **”**
C.H. Spurgeon

Here we find detailed accounts of Jesus' teaching. He is presented as the King who speaks with authority to His people.

Mark
This was probably the first Gospel to be written, and it may well have been written for the Romans. Its emphasis on deeds rather than words is something the practically-minded Romans would appreciate. It contains very few parables, but many accounts of the miracles of Jesus. He is portrayed here as the mighty Son of God, with absolute authority over both creatures and creation.

Luke
Luke writes to convince Theophilus and other Greeks that Jesus is the Christ (1:1-4). His Gospel abounds with instances of how the Saviour showed mercy to the less privileged and the social

outcast, and illustrates particularly His compassion towards women and children. In Luke's account we see the God of glory coming down to our level. He enters into our condition and is subject to our circumstances; yet in all this He remains without sin.

In many ways these first three Gospels are very similar. They are known as the 'synoptic' Gospels, because they give a 'common view' of the life and teaching of Jesus.

John
John's Gospel was the last to be written (about AD 90), and it goes more deeply than the others into the meaning and significance of the life and death of Jesus. John's purpose in writing is stated very clearly: *'But these are written that you may believe that Jesus is the Christ, the Son of God, and that by believing you may have life in his name'* (20:31).

“ *In distinction from the Synoptics, John's Gospel discusses not so much the kingdom as the King Himself; reveals that Jesus from the very beginning asserted His Messianic claim; describes, with few exceptions, Christ's work*

A carpenter's shop in Nazareth.   ▶

in Judea; dwells at great length on the events and discourses which belong to a period of less than twenty-four hours; unmistakably indicates that the active ministry of our Lord extended over a period of at least three years; and, in *general, places great emphasis upon the spiritual character of Christ's task on earth. Nevertheless, John and the Synoptics, far from contradicting one another, supplement each other.* **99**
William Hendriksen

A carved ark near the synagogue at Capernaum. The original ark of the covenant was made by the people of Israel at Sinai (see Exodus 25:10-22). It was a wooden chest, which contained the two stone tablets of the Ten Commandments. Its lid was the mercy seat, which symbolized the presence of God among His people.

Acts

This book covers a period of about thirty years and is a thrilling account of the birth and growth of the church. Blessings and problems go hand in hand, and both are used by the Holy Spirit to accomplish God's purposes.

AD 30	The birth of the church	Acts 1-2
AD 34	Paul's conversion	Acts 9
AD 46-47	First missionary tour	Acts 13-14
AD 48	Council at Jerusalem	Acts 15
AD 48-51	Second missionary tour	Acts 15:36-18:22
AD 53	Start of third missionary tour	Acts 18:23
AD 54-57	Paul's ministry at Ephesus	Acts 19
AD 57-58	Paul in Greece	Acts 20
AD 58	Back to Jerusalem	Acts 21
AD 58-60	In prison at Caesarea	Acts 24-26
AD 60-61	Voyage to Rome	Acts 27-28

—— Teaching ——

The remaining twenty-two books provide us with the teaching that we need in order to understand the Christian faith and live the Christian life. They bring us both doctrine and comfort. All but one of them are letters written to churches or individuals: of these, thirteen were written by Paul; the letter to the Hebrews has no named author, and the others were written by James and Jude (one each), Peter (two) and John (three).

As the gospel spread and churches were formed, the need for teaching and instruction became clear. Some churches were having great difficulties with false teachers and their false doctrines (for example, in Galatia and Colossae). Others had internal problems arising from wrong attitudes and behaviour among their members (for example, at Corinth and Thessalonica). These and many other problems needed to be dealt with, and so the New Testament letters were written.

The new churches were very vulnerable to heresy, and the apostles' letters warned them of this danger and condemned false teachers in the strongest possible way (see, for example, Galatians 1:6-9; Philippians 3:2; 2 Peter 2:12-22; 2 John 7-11, Jude 4). The strength of the condemnation indicates the importance the New Testament writers attached to doctrinal purity.

But if a church's doctrine is important, so too is the purity of its life and behaviour. The church at Corinth had gone sadly astray here, and 1 Corinthians was

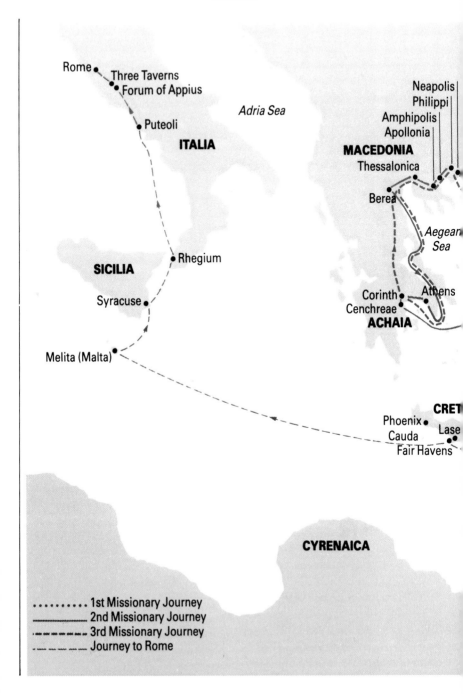

Rome
Three Taverns
Forum of Appius
Puteoli
Adria Sea
ITALIA
Neapolis
Philippi
Amphipolis
Apollonia
MACEDONIA
Thessalonica
Berea
Aegean Sea
Rhegium
SICILIA
Syracuse
Corinth
Cenchreae
Athens
ACHAIA
Melita (Malta)
CRET
Phoenix
Cauda
Lase
Fair Havens
CYRENAICA

•••••••••• 1st Missionary Journey
————— 2nd Missionary Journey
—·—·—· 3rd Missionary Journey
— — — Journey to Rome

THE JOURNEYS OF
THE APOSTLE PAUL

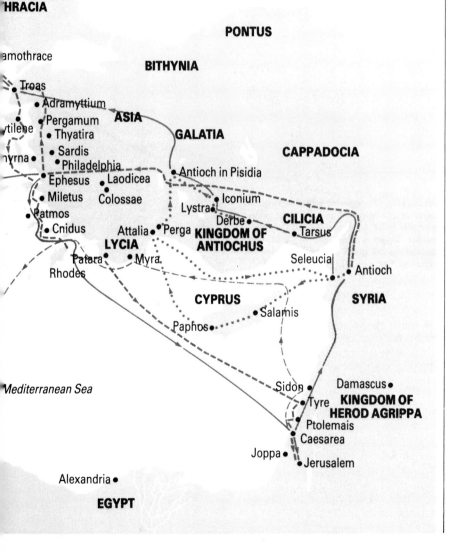

Euxine Sea

PONTUS

BITHYNIA

HRACIA

amothrace

Troas

Adramyttium

Pergamum
Thyatira

ASIA

GALATIA

CAPPADOCIA

tilene

Sardis

Philadelphia

yrna

Ephesus • Laodicea

Antioch in Pisidia

Miletus
Colossae

Lystra

Iconium

CILICIA

Patmos

Derbe

Tarsus

Cnidus

Attalia • Perga **KINGDOM OF
ANTIOCHUS**

LYCIA

Patara

Myra

Seleucia

Rhodes

Antioch

CYPRUS

SYRIA

Paphos

Salamis

Mediterranean Sea

Sidon

Damascus •

Tyre **KINGDOM OF
HEROD AGRIPPA**

Ptolemais

Caesarea

Joppa •

Jerusalem

Alexandria •

EGYPT

Winnowing. Farmers in some remote parts of the Middle East still toss grain into the air to separate chaff from the wheat. Christ is described by John the Baptist as the great Winnower, who will separate the evil from the good.

written to put this right. Here Paul

66 takes the lid off one of the early churches, and gives us a fascinating glimpse of the none too edifying contents. 99
The Lion Handbook to the Bible

Some of the letters were written to encourage younger men in the ministry (1 and 2 Timothy, Titus), and others were more general and not addressed to any specific problem. Paul's letters to the Romans and the Ephesians come into this category, and these two letters contain some of the richest

It will be helpful to see the order in which the New Testament books were written. The following is a possible order, though it is impossible to be specific about dates:

AD 40-50 James
AD 50-54 Galatians, 1 & 2 Thessalonians
AD 55-60 1 and 2 Corinthians, Romans, Mark
AD 60-65 Colossians, Philemon, Ephesians, Philippians
AD 65-70 1 & 2 Timothy, Titus, Jude, Hebrews, 1 & 2 Peter, Matthew, Luke, Acts
AD 90- John, 1, 2 & 3 John, Revelation

theological teaching in the New Testament.

To these must be added the encouragement of 1 Peter, the practical and down-to-earth teaching of James, the glory of Christ's superiority as seen in Hebrews, and so on. Each letter is different, but complementary to the rest, and all blend together to form the unsurpassed beauty of the New Testament.

*** The letters of Paul differ widely among themselves. The Epistle to the Romans is almost a systematic exposition of the plan of salvation. Philemon is concerned with a little personal matter between Paul and one of his converts. But even where Paul is most theological he is personal, he is faithful to his theology. Theology to him is never separate from experience, and experience*

—— Enemies of the Gospel ——

The Herod Family

Herod the Great	King when Jesus was born.
Herod Antipas	Son of Herod the Great. It was this Herod who executed John the Baptist.
Herod Agrippa I	Grandson of Herod the Great. This is the Herod who executed James and imprisoned Peter (Acts 12).
Herod Agrippa II	Son of Agrippa I. The last of the Herods, of whom we read in Acts 25.

Pharisees

They were a party which originated in the second century BC. In New Testament times they exercised great power, although they were only about 6,000 in number. They laid great stress upon keeping the law in every detail. They would not eat with non-Pharisees and generally held themselves aloof from others. It was their arrogant self-righteousness that brought them into continual conflict with Jesus. He denounced them as hypocrites. The scribes were themselves Pharisees.

Sadducees

The Sadducees were the other main party of New Testament times. They did not have as much influence over the people as did the Pharisees, though they dominated the Sanhedrin (the Jewish ruling court). The fact that they were drawn mainly from rich land-owning families may account for their lack of popular support. They did not believe in angels or in the resurrection of the dead (Acts 23:8). Nearly all the Sadducees were priests, and many of the high priests came from this party.

The theatre at Ephesus, which was the scene of the riot by silversmiths described in Acts 19.

never separate from theology. Even petty problems he settles always in the light of eternal principles. Hence his letters, though the specific circumstances that gave rise to them are past and gone, will never be antiquated. "
J. Gresham Machen

The book of Revelation stands on its own. In symbolic language it issues a clear call to Christians to face suffering in the knowledge that Jesus is on the throne.

—— Parables ——

Jesus often used parables as a means of teaching. A parable, according to the old definition, is 'an earthly story with a heavenly meaning'. Jesus never used fantasy or fiction; he painted word-pictures of everyday activities and told stories about familiar things to which people could easily relate. Normally a parable conveys one basic message; it is dangerous to try to interpret every detail in a spiritual way.

" *They are stories and examples from the world in which Jesus lived, and they are told in order to convey a spiritual truth by means of a single point of comparison. The details of the story are supportive of the message the parable conveys. They should not be given a point-by-point analysis and interpreted as an allegory, for then they lose their significance.* "
Simon Kistemaker

It is not true to say that Jesus always used parables to make difficult truths easy to understand. The fact is that some of the parables are not easy to interpret.

For instance, the parable of the Sower (Mark 4:2-20) is well known to us and its interpretation is clear. But the disciples who first heard the story did not understand it and had to ask Jesus what it meant. Without Christ's interpretation that parable would have remained a mystery.

Why then did Jesus use parables? He Himself gives one reason to His disciples in the passage in question:

" *The secret of the kingdom of God has been given to you. But to those on the outside everything is said in parables so that 'they may be ever seeing but never perceiving, and ever hearing but never understanding; otherwise they might turn and be forgiven!'* "
Mark 4:11-12

Inside an old synagogue. This one is at Nazareth. The word 'synagogue' means 'a place of meeting'. After their return from exile in Babylon, the Jews began to establish synagogues as places where they could meet together to study the law of God. ▶

This is an amazing answer. Does it mean that Jesus is deliberately hiding the truth from people so that they will not repent and receive forgiveness? The comments of Charles Spurgeon on these verses is helpful:

66 *The usual reasons for the use of parables would be to make truth clear, to arrest attention, and to impress teaching upon the*

The modern Great Jerusalem Synagogue.

—— New Testament Parables ——

	Matthew	Mark	Luke
Salt	5:13		14:34-35
Light	5:14-15	4:21-22	8:16
Two builders	7:24-27		6:47-49
Garments and wineskins	9:16-17	2:21-22	5:36-38
Sower	13:3-8	4:3-8	8:5-8
Weeds	13:24-30		
Mustard seed	13:31-32	4:30-32	13:18-19
Yeast	13:33		13:20-21
Treasure hidden in a field	13:44		
Fine pearls	13:45-46		
Net full of fish	13:47-48		
Lost sheep	18:10-14		15:4-7
Unmerciful servant	18:23-34		
Workers in the vineyard	20:1-16		
Two sons	21:28-32		
Tenants	21:33-46	12:1-12	20:9-19
Wedding banquet	22:1-14		
Fig tree	24:32-35	13:28-31	21:29-33
Ten virgins	25:1-13		
Talents	25:14-30		
Sheep and goats	25:31-46		
Growing seed		4:26-29	
Two debtors			7:41-43
Good Samaritan			10:25-37
Friend at midnight			11:5-8
Rich fool			12:13-21
Watchfulness			12:35-41
Wise manager			12:42-48
Barren fig tree			13:6-9
Wedding feast			14:7-14
Great banquet			14:15-24
Counting the cost			14:28-33
Lost coin			15:8-10
Lost son			15:11-32
Shrewd manager			16:1-9
Rich man and Lazarus			16:19-31
Farmer and servant			17:7-10
Persistent widow			18:1-8
Pharisee and the tax collector			18:9-14
Ten minas (pounds)			19:11-27

The barren landscape near the road from Jerusalem to Jericho. This was the setting for the parable of the Good Samaritan.

memory. But in this instance our Lord was, by His parabolic speech, fulfilling the judicial sentence which had been long before pronounced upon the apostate nation among whom He received such unworthy treatment. They had become so morally and spiritually diseased, that the only thing they would notice was the attractive dress of a truth: for the truth itself they had no liking and no perception. Those who refuse to see are punished by becoming unable to see. The penalty of sin is to be left in sin. The Jews of our Lord's day would trifle with what they heard, and so they were left to hear without understanding. 99

The parables of Jesus are part of God's revealed truth, and contain rich and glorious teaching for us. The passage in Mark 4 must be seen in its context. In the previous chapter Jesus was confronted by the most stubborn and unreasonable unbelief. He is even accused of doing the devil's work. As John Calvin puts it, such people must *'endure the blame of their own blindness and hardness'.*

We are to read the parables, believe them, and in faith seek to understand their meaning as the Holy Spirit gives us light.

——— New Testament Miracles ———

	Matthew	Mark	Luke	John
Leper	8:1-4	1:40-45	5:12-15	
Centurion's servant	8:5-13		7:1-10	
Peter's mother-in-law	8:14-15	1:30-31	4:38-39	
Stilling the storm	8:23-27	4:35-41	8:22-25	
Legion	8:28-34	5:1-15	8:27-35	
Paralytic	9:1-8	2:1-12	5:17-26	
Jairus' daughter	9:18-26	5:21-43	8:41-56	
Woman with haemorrhage	9:20-22	5:25-29	8:43-48	
Two blind men	9:27-31			
Demon-possessed man	9:32-33			
Man with the shrivelled hand	12:9-13	3:1-5	6:6-11	
Blind and dumb man	12:22		11:14	
Feeding of 5000	14:15-21	6:35-44	9:12-17	6:5-14
Walking on water	14:25	6:48-51		6:19-21
Canaanite woman's daughter	15:21-28	7:24-30		
Feeding of 4000	15:32-39	8:1-9		
Epileptic boy	17:14-21	9:14-29	9:37-42	
Coin in fish's mouth	17:24-27			
Bartimaeus	20:29-34	10:46-52	18:35-43	
The fig tree withers	21:17-22	11:12-14 11:20-26		
Drives out an evil spirit		1:23-26	4:33-36	
Deaf and dumb man		7:31-37		
Blind man at Bethsaida		8:22-26		
Catch of fish			5:1-11	
Widow of Nain's son			7:11-16	
Crippled woman			13:10-17	
Man with dropsy			14:1-6	
Ten lepers			17:11-19	
Malchus' ear			22:49-51	
Water to wine				2:1-11
Boy at Capernaum				4:46-54
Pool of Bethesda				5:1-16
Man born blind				9:1-8
Lazarus				11:1-45
Another catch of fish				21:1-14

Recommended Books

The Lion Handbook to the Bible: David and Pat Alexander (Lion Publishing)
Handbook of Life in Bible Times: J A Thompson (Inter-Varsity Press)
Survey of the Bible: William Hendriksen (Evangelical Press)

Jensen's Survey of the Old Testament: Irving L Jensen (Moody Press)
The New Testament — An Introduction to its Literature and History: J Gresham Machen (Banner of Truth Trust)
Nothing but the Truth: Brian Edwards (Evangelical Press)

PART TWO
THE CHURCH

The history of the Christian church is a
thrilling and exciting story of God's dealings with His
people. There are times when we see the church
turning from the truth on which it was founded.
A period of struggle then begins and it seems as if
Christianity is about to die out altogether. At other
times the story is quite different: the Bible is believed
and preached with boldness. As a result, the church
enjoys spiritual strength and vigour.

*« The history of the Church is simply an account of
its success and its failure in carrying out Christ's great
commission to 'go into all the world, and preach the
gospel to every creature' and 'teach all nations'. »*
A.M. Renwick

All Christians should know something of this story.
The short account which follows has been written to
give new believers some idea of the great church to
which they now belong. To cover 2,000 years of
history in so short a space is an almost impossible
task. Inevitably, much has had to be omitted, but an
attempt has been made to deal with the main events
and characters.

5
The first 450 years

The birth and early growth of the Christian church are recorded for us in the Acts of the Apostles. We see there the blessings and difficulties that the church experienced in the first thirty or so years of its history. In those early years most of the opposition came from the Jews, but in the second half of the century the situation was to change dramatically.

Persecution

In AD 64 the great fire of Rome raged for nine days and damaged the city severely. The emperor Nero was suspected of causing the fire, and so, to protect himself, he blamed the Christians. There followed the first Roman persecution of the church. Believers were subjected to inhuman cruelties: some were crucified; others were sewn up in skins of wild animals and torn to pieces by dogs; others were smeared with pitch and set ablaze to be used as human torches.

From time to time over the next 250 years the Roman Empire inflicted many such persecutions upon the Christian church. They varied in intensity according to

The Roman Emperor Nero (54-68 AD) was one of the cruellest persecutors of the early church.

who was emperor at the time. Under the reign of Domitian (AD 81-96) the persecution was particularly severe. It was during this period that John was exiled to the island of Patmos. Even under a relatively tolerant emperor like Trajan, things were not easy. For instance, when Pliny became governor of Bithynia in AD 111, he found that Christianity was spreading rapidly in the area. Being very concerned about this *'depraved and extravagant superstition',* as he called it, he wrote to Trajan explaining how he dealt with Christians:

66 *This is the course that I have adopted . . . I ask them if they are Christians. If they admit it I repeat the question a second and a third time, threatening capital punishment; if they persist I sentence them to death. For . . . their . . . inflexible obstinacy should certainly be punished. There were others . . . whom I reserved to be sent to Rome, since they were Roman citizens. All who denied that they were . . . Christians I considered should be discharged . . . especially because they cursed Christ, a thing which, it is said, genuine Christians cannot be induced to do.* **99**

The year AD 248 marked the thousandth anniversary of the foundation of Rome and awakened fresh enthusiasm for Roman traditions and religion. This inevitably caused problems for the Christians, and after eleven years of peace the emperor Decius launched a vicious persecution against them. He believed that the old Roman virtues could only be restored by returning to the old Roman gods. The church therefore became a prime target, and he was determined to kill off the Christian faith once and for all.

The last persecution began in AD 303 during the reign of Diocletian, when an order was given to destroy all Christian places of worship and to burn all Christian books.

Martyrs

These persecutions produced many martyrs, but they did not succeed in checking the spread of Christianity. In fact, they had the opposite effect, for while many nominal Christians did succumb and deny the faith, the way in which most believers faced their ordeal was a tremendously powerful witness to the pagan onlookers. It was said at the time that 'the blood of the martyrs is the seed of the church', and this was undoubtedly true.

☐ **Ignatius** was born in about AD 40. He was a very gifted man, who eventually became bishop of the church at Antioch. He was condemned to be thrown to the lions in the Colosseum at Rome. As a result, he had to make a journey, which took six weeks over land and sea, to go to Rome and to his death. There between about AD 110 and 117 he was 'butchered to make a Roman holiday'. He faced the lions with remarkable courage, saying:

66 *I am God's grain, to be ground between the teeth of wild beasts, so that I may become a holy loaf for the Lord.* **99**

☐ **Polycarp** was bishop of Smyrna. About AD 156 he

The Colosseum, Rome. Dedicated in AD 80, this huge amphitheatre could hold about 45,000 spectators. In the days of the Roman Empire it was here that many Christians were thrown to the lions and bears.

suffered a martyr's death at the age of 86. When he was given the usual opportunity to acknowledge publicly the deity of the Roman emperor and to curse Christ, the old man replied:

❝ *Eighty-six years have I served Him, and He has done me no wrong: how then can I blaspheme my King who saved me? . . . You threaten the fire that burns for an hour, and after a little while is quenched; for you are ignorant of the fire of the judgement to come, and of everlasting punishment . . . Do what you wish.* **❞**

He was burnt at the stake.

The list of martyrs is endless — Justin, Perpetua, Cyprian, and so on. They were treated with unbelievable cruelty; yet still the church grew. The truth is that the greatest enemy of the early church was not persecution, but heresy.

Heresy

☐ **Gnosticism** was a far-reaching heresy that touched almost every church in the Roman Empire. Its influence was wide and long-lasting, threatening at one time to obliterate the Christian faith. The name 'Gnostic' is

❝ *an umbrella-term to include all those of this period who professed*

A thirteenth-century copy of a Syriac Bible. Syriac was the language of a version of the Bible produced in the fourth century AD and used in many eastern churches. In the fifth century some Syriac-speaking churches fell victim to a heresy which emphasized Christ's deity at the expense of His humanity.

to have some secret revelation or knowledge, and it contains within its range both those on the borders of mainstream Christianity and those whose doctrine was mainly pagan mysticism garnished with a few Christian ideas and phrases. **"**
M.A. Smith

Gnostics claimed to have a secret or hidden 'knowledge', and they thought they could combine Christianity with other religions and ideas of the world.

" *Gnostisicm was an immense peril for the church. It cut out the historic foundations of Christianity. Its God is not the God of the Old Testament, which is the work of an inferior or even evil being. Its Christ had no real incarnation, death or resurrection. Its salvation is for the few capable of spiritual enlightenment. The peril was the greater because Gnosticism was represented by some of the keenest minds in the church of the second century.* **"**
W. Walker

☐ The heresy of **Montanism** arose as a strong reaction against Gnosticism. It spoke out against the lack of spiritual life in the church and emphasized the ministry of the Holy Spirit, particularly in the realm of prophecy. This was an emphasis which the church needed. Unfortunately, the Montanists fell into the same trap into which many other such movements have fallen down the centuries — they placed human speculation above

the authority of Scripture. Hand in hand with this went a consuming spiritual pride. Montanism in its turn also provoked a strong reaction, and this was in many ways the greatest damage that it did.

" *The Montanists had also brought impassioned preaching into disrepute, together with all forms of emotionalism in religion. Preaching virtually ceased for many centuries. A direct result of this was that the priest was magnified because he ministered the awe-inspiring mysteries of the altar and it was supposed that only through him could men do business with God. Outside of the church where he ministered there was no salvation. It was a sad departure from the faith of the apostolic church, even though the priests vociferously claimed to be in the apostolic succession.* **"**
A.M. Renwick

Gnosticism and Montanism were at their peak in the second century. In the fourth and fifth centuries two other heresies arose which had a more lasting influence upon the church.

☐ **Arianism.** Arius was a presbyter in Alexandria. In about AD 318 he began to teach that Christ was created and had no existence before His birth in Bethlehem. He was thus denying the deity of the Lord Jesus. He was removed from office in AD 321, but he had a strong following. In 325 the First General Council of the church was

called at Nicea to deal with the problem. Here Athanasius defended the biblical position and Arius defended his heresy. At the Council of Constantinople in AD 381 the famous Nicene creed was produced containing the following denunciation of Arianism:

" *We believe . . . in one Lord Jesus Christ, the only-begotten Son of God, begotten of the Father before all the ages, Light of Light, true God of true God, begotten not made, of one substance with the Father.* **"**

Arianism was then officially outlawed as heresy.

☐ **Pelagianism.** Pelagius was a British monk who laid great emphasis upon the human will. He denied the doctrine of original sin and taught that man had the ability not to sin, if he so wished.

" *Man, he claimed, is not born sinful, but is able to do all that God requires of him, if he only wills to do so. Pelagius taught that the ability to be saved is found in the lost sinner's heart if he will but use it. He really denied the*

◄

'Pompey's Pillar' at Alexandria, Egypt. It was erected by Diocletian to serve as a landmark from the sea. Alexandria was one of the greatest cities of the ancient world. The early Christian church there was blessed with many famous leaders such as Clement, Origen and Athanasius. The growth of the Arian heresy in the church at Alexandria may have been one reason for its eventual decline.

necessity for a 'birth from above', for the inward work of the Holy Spirit, and for the intervention of the unmerited grace of God. Salvation is 'not of works lest any man should boast' (Eph. 2:9) but Pelagius's teachings were virtually a denial of this great truth. **"**
S.M. Houghton

One of the greatest opponents of heresy was **Augustine.** Born in North Africa in AD 354, Augustine was converted at the age of thirty-one. He became bishop of Hippo in North Africa, and there he wrote many books. In his famous *Confessions* he gave his personal testimony of salvation, but his more important works were probably his books on sin and grace which he wrote specifically to deal with Pelagianism. He died in AD 430.

Conversion of Constantine

Persecutions and heresies plagued the church and did great damage, but perhaps the greatest damage was done by the so-called conversion of Constantine. This man was locked in battle with his rival Maxentius for the throne of the Roman Empire. The historian Eusebius tells us that before the crucial battle at the Milvian Bridge outside Rome on 27 October 312, Constantine saw in the sky a vision of a flaming cross with the words inscribed in Greek, 'By this sign conquer'. He put the sign of the cross on his soldiers' equipment and gained a great victory. He was convinced that the Christians' God had given him the victory and he now professed to being a Christian.

Whether Constantine was truly converted is open to serious doubt, but the Christian church was never the same again. It now had the official support of the Roman emperor, and while this certainly brought privileges (the greatest of these being the end of persecution), the price was enormous. Previously, to be a Christian had involved great hardship; but now, to become a member of the church brought great social and political advantages. The result was that thousands joined the church who had had no experience of the new birth, and though the church grew much stronger in numerical terms, it was spiritually much weaker. Days of persecution were replaced by days of spiritual slackness and worldliness. The simplicity of earlier Christian worship gave way to the pomp and ceremony of pagan court practices. Constantine himself liked to dress in rich, ornate robes, and he presented a similar set of garments to the bishop of Jerusalem. Thus vestments were introduced for the first time, and other things like the use of candles and pilgrimages infiltrated Christianity from the pagan ceremonies of the court.

The Milvian Bridge, Rome, where Constantine fought and won an all-important battle against his rival Maxentius.

Worse still, it now became a political advantage to be a church leader:

66 *Even the church in the capital city, Rome, was not to be untroubled. The leadership of this great church was too big a prize, and many battles were fought over who should be bishop . . . before the fourth century was over, thoughtful pagans were to express horror as street battles raged and left piles of dead, while the clergy fought each other for the right to be pastor of the Roman church.* **99**
M.A. Smith

However, it was not a time of total gloom. The freedom that Christians now enjoyed allowed churches to be built, and missionary work expanded.

66 *It is pointless to speculate over what might have happened if Constantine had lost the Battle of the Milvian Bridge outside Rome. The driving force among the Christians, even allowing for their many imperfections, was strong enough to have obtained toleration before long. Christianity did not need imperial backing, as is shown by the fact that the churches survived the collapse of the Western Empire within a century of their having been freed from persecution. With all the faults, there was enough of the Spirit of Christ still among the church leaders and members to ensure that the organization would continue in spite of political upheaval.* **99**
M.A. Smith

6
The Middle Ages

The next thousand years were justifiably known as the Dark Ages. Biblical Christianity was at a low ebb, and the period saw the rise of papal authority. The seeds of this had been sown when Constantine linked the church with the state, and it was given a fresh impetus by Leo (390-461) when he became bishop of Rome in 440.

Leo was a man of great ability who set out to establish the church of Rome as supreme over all other churches. He argued, as no one had done before, that by His words in Matthew 16:18 Jesus had singled out Peter and given him authority over all the apostles. Since Peter had been the first bishop of Rome, he declared, that authority now belonged to all succeeding bishops of that church. According to Roman Catholic tradition, Peter was bishop of Rome from AD 42 to 67; yet there is no mention of it in the Acts of the Apostles which covers this period, nor is there any historical evidence to substantiate it. Nevertheless, Leo persisted in his claim, and the emperor Valentinian III gave him his support. When eventually the Roman Empire crumbled, instead of this myth being buried as one might have expected, the position of the Roman bishop was enhanced.

❝ Leo the Great died in 461, having used his time as bishop of Rome to transform the Roman see from being merely one of the four great patriarchates to being the potential leader of Christendom. The foundations of the mediaeval papacy had already been laid.❞
M.A. Smith

Succeeding bishops of Rome built on the foundation that Leo had laid. This was especially true of Gregory, who was bishop of Rome from 590-604. Known as 'Gregory the Great', he was really the first pope, as we understand the title today.

The Celtic Church
In AD 596 Gregory decided to send to Britain a monk named Augustine to Christianize the country. In the following year he landed with forty of his followers at the Isle of Thanet in Kent, and established his headquarters at Canterbury. Yet there was already

a strong Celtic church in Britain, and it had been there for centuries. Tertullian, writing in the third century, mentions Christians in Britain. Furthermore, the year that Augustine landed was the year in which Columba died on the island of Iona after a lifetime of evangelism in Scotland and Ireland.

We do not know how Christianity came to Britain, but there are several fascinating legends:

☐ It was brought here by the apostle Paul himself. This story is based on a statement by Clement of Rome that Paul preached to the furthermost limits of the west.

☐ The apostle Philip sent Joseph of Arimathaea to establish Christianity here, and he made his headquarters at Glastonbury. This legend was probably manufactured by the monks at Glastonbury.

☐ The first person to preach Christ to Britons was Brân the Blessed, a famous character in Welsh mythology.

Whatever the truth may be about Christianity reaching Britain, we do know for certain that at the Council of Arles in 314 there were British representatives. Further, by the time Gregory decided to 'Christianize' Britain, the country had already been blessed by the

St Augustine's cross at Ebbsfleet in the Isle of Thanet, Kent. The cross was erected in 1884 to mark the spot where Augustine first landed in Britain. It was here that he met and preached to King Ethelbert of Kent.

ministries of men such as Alban in England, Patrick in Ireland, Ninian and Columba in Scotland, and David in Wales. The Celtic church was strongly independent of Rome.

" *The efforts of Augustin to bring the leaders of the Celtic church into the Roman communion which he represented completely failed, for they clung passionately to their independence. He died in 604, having barely succeeded in extending the Roman Church beyond Kent. His importance lies in having established Canterbury Cathedral, the influence of which spread later throughout all the land.* **"**
A.M. Renwick

The Holy Roman Empire

In the eighth century the Roman church was facing serious trouble. The Lombards were threatening invasion from without, and there was a growing rebellion within. The papacy turned for help to the king of the Franks. So began a close relationship between the Frankish kings and the Roman popes that led ultimately to the crowning of Charlemagne, on Christmas Day 800, as Holy Roman Emperor.

" *This act was the coping-stone on the edifice of mediaeval Christendom. The Christian church had changed from being a gathered company of believers. It was now a political entity with a visible emperor. But behind the emperor stood the spiritual and political*

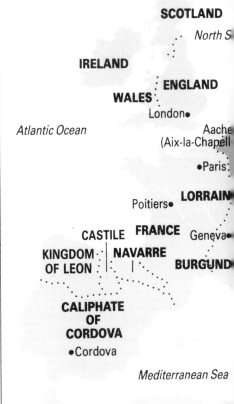

power and prestige of the pope of Rome, soon to assert itself over even the civil power. **"**
M.A. Smith

Charlemagne was a strong ruler. He vigorously maintained his authority over the pope as well as everyone else. He was conscious that he had been crowned by a pope, and that this might appear

EUROPE IN THE TENTH CENTURY

NMARK

Baltic Sea

SAXONY

POLAND

RUSSIA

ankfurt

Vorms BOHEMIA

OLY ROMAN

BAVARIA

HUNGARY

EMPIRE

CROATIA

Danube

Black Sea

SERBIA

PAPAL
STATES Adriatic
Rome● Sea

BULGARIA

●Constantinople

KINGDOM
OF
ITALY

BYZANTINE EMPIRE

to give the pope a certain superiority. So it is probably significant that when his son Louis became emperor with him in 813, there was no pope present at the ceremony. None the less, Charlemagne had greatly strengthened the power of the papacy, and in later years this power was ruthlessly applied.

When Hildebrand became pope as Gregory VII in 1073, the long desire of the Roman church to gain total supremacy was to receive partial fulfilment. Hildebrand's objective was not only the supremacy of the church over the state, but also the supremacy of the pope over both state and church. His ambition brought him into direct conflict with the Holy Roman Emperor Henry IV. A disagreement between the two men resulted in the pope demanding that the emperor appear before him in Rome. When Henry refused and then declared that Hildebrand was no longer pope, Hildebrand retaliated by excommunicating Henry and pronouncing an interdict against his subjects. Excommunication meant that no one was allowed to have anything to do with Henry. The interdict declared that churches in his realm were closed, and no marriage or funeral services could be performed. The pressure on Henry was enormous, and he had to give in.

66 What followed is one of the most notable events in the history of Europe. With his wife and child Henry set out in midwinter to cross the Alps, braving all the discomforts of wind and weather, to present himself at the feet of the Pope. He found Gregory at Canossa, a stronghold of Countess Matilda of Tuscany. But the Pope refused to admit him to his presence. He intended to humble the Emperor to the dust. In the cold and snow of winter, and on three successive days, Henry stood with bare feet and the white garment of a penitent, in the snow of the courtyard of the castle, waiting for the Pope to grant him permission to kneel at his feet and ask forgiveness. On the fourth day the Pope consented to receive him, and the sentence of excommunication and the interdict were removed. 99
S.M. Houghton

Seven years later Henry raised an army and overthrew Hildebrand, but the fact remained that the head of the Holy Roman Empire had been humiliated by the power of the pope.

66 If [Hildebrand's] methods were worldly and unscrupulous, as they undoubtedly were, no misfortune ever caused him to abate his claims, and even in apparent defeat he won a moral victory. The ideals that he had established for the papacy were to live long after him. 99
W. Walker

Papal Power

The power of the papacy was occasionally challenged by rulers like Frederick Barbarossa of Germany, who became Holy Roman Emperor, and King Henry II of England, but under the popes Innocent III (1198-1216) and Boniface VIII (1294-1303) it grew from strength to strength. Innocent III declared that no king had the right to rule unless he served the papacy with reverence and full submission.

The church's increased political power contrasted strongly with the growing spiritual weakness that accompanied its rejection of biblical truths. Doctrines completely alien to Scripture were invented, and these have become an integral part of Roman Catholic dogma. They include transubstantiation (the changing of the bread and wine of the sacrament into the very body and blood of Christ), purgatory, prayers for the dead and the adoration of Mary.

The palace of the popes at Avignon, France.

Teachers of false doctrine can never tolerate the truth, so to enforce the acceptance of official dogma the Inquisition was established.

It is often said that power corrupts, and this was certainly the case with the papacy. Some of the popes of this era were notorious for their wickedness; indeed, John XXIII was forced to resign because of his 'destestable unseemly life and manners'. The influence of the papacy began to wane, especially when for forty years (1378-1417) there were two popes, one in Avignon and the other in Rome.

❝ *Some nations supported the pope at Avignon, some the pope at Rome. So serious was this schism that the power of Rome was never the same again. Catholics had believed that their salvation depended on acknowledging the successor of Peter. Here were two popes for nearly forty years, each anathematizing the other, and each claiming to be the only true occupant of Peter's chair. No wonder the Catholic world was perplexed.* **❞**
A.M. Renwick

But into the awful spiritual darkness of this time some glimmers of light began to shine.

Peter Waldo.

The Waldenses

In about the year 1170 God began to deal with a man named Peter Waldo, who lived in the city of Lyons in France. He employed two men to translate the four Gospels and other parts of the New Testament from Latin into French. As he read these, his mind was filled with biblical truths which he found impossible to keep to himself. He was joined by others, and the Waldenses (or Waldensians) began to travel round the country preaching the gospel. The missionary zeal of these believers was astounding: by 1200, they had churches in Spain, Italy, Switzerland and Germany; by 1300, they were in Austria,

Hungary, Poland, Bohemia and the Netherlands.

Rome could not tolerate this, and forbade them to preach. Indeed, the Council of Valencia (1229) prohibited men who were not priests from reading the Scriptures and the Bible itself was placed on the list of forbidden books. When this did not silence the Waldensians, the full force of the Inquisition was used against them. Thousands were tortured and killed, but the light had begun to shine.

John Wycliffe

John Wycliffe was a student at Balliol College, Oxford, and gradually earned a great reputation as one of the ablest scholars in the University. He was a priest in the Roman Catholic Church, but he rejected transubstantiation, criticized the doctrine of purgatory, and generally expressed great dissatisfaction with the church. This naturally brought him into conflict with the bishops, but he was very popular with the common people, and also enjoyed the protection of John of Gaunt, the king's son.

66 No small element in Wyclif's power was that he was thought to have no scholastic equal in contemporary England. Men hesitated to cross intellectual swords with him. Equally conspicuous were his intense patriotism and his deep piety. He voiced the popular resentment of foreign papal taxation and greed,

and the popular longing for a simpler, more Biblical faith. **99**
W. Walker

Wycliffe has been called 'the morning star of the Reformation', and that is undoubtedly a worthy title. In his questioning of the whole structure of the Roman church he was led to do two vitally important things. First, he organized bands of preachers known as the Lollards, who travelled the country preaching the Word of God. This was, by and large, the only instruction the people had in the things of God. Secondly, this remarkable man was responsible for the first Bible in the English language.

66 *As translator of the Bible and upholder of its supreme authority he adopted the Waldensian Scriptural standpoint, fortified it with learning and logic, and enabled men more fully to judge for themselves how far the Church and her creed harmonized with the spirit and teaching of Christ.* **99**
Henry Cowan

Wycliffe died at Lutterworth in 1384. Forty years later the Roman church dug up his bones, burned them, and scattered the ashes on the River Swift which runs through the town. It was a bitter but futile gesture. Wycliffe's work was done, and the Reformation would see the full harvest of the seed he had sown.

Jan Hus
Wycliffe's writings had a great effect upon Jan Hus, who was

John Wycliffe sends out his 'poor preachers' with his English translation of the Bible.

Rector of Prague University in Bohemia. Hus was a great preacher. He was popular with the common people but hated by the church authorities. His books were burned, and he himself was excommunicated by the pope. He was ordered to appear before the Council of Constance in 1414 and, being promised safe conduct by the emperor, he went.

“ He was thrown into prison and barbarously treated. The emperor gave an order for his release but was terrified into cancelling it by the pope and cardinals. After seven months of cruel suffering Hus was put through a mockery of a trial. His defence was drowned with shouts of 'Recant, Recant!' He declared he would detract nothing unless it was contrary to God's Word. In 1415, after the most shameful degradation by the Council, he was burnt at their request outside Constance by the civil authorities. ”
A.M. Renwick

The thousand-year darkness was beginning to be penetrated by lights such as Wycliffe and Hus. In the providence of God, a very significant discovery was also made at this time. The invention of printing in the second half of the fifteenth century resulted in copies of the Bible being printed and circulated. This gave a great incentive for the translation of the Bible for the first time into the various European languages. An Italian version appeared in 1474, a Bohemian (i.e. Czech) version in 1475, Dutch and French in 1477, and Spanish in 1478. The ground was being prepared for the coming Reformation.

A square in the centre of Prague.

7
The Reformation

The only true reformation is that which emanates from the Word of God. The Holy Scriptures, by bearing witness to the incarnation, death, and resurrection of the Son of God, create in man by the Holy Ghost a faith which justifies him. That faith which produces in him a new life, unites him to Christ, without his requiring a chain of bishops or a Roman mediator, who would separate him from the Saviour instead of drawing him nearer. This reformation by the Word *restores that spiritual Christianity which the outward and hierarchical religion destroys; and from the regeneration of individuals naturally results the regeneration of the church.*

Merle d'Aubigné

All that we have seen so far has shown the desperate need of the church for reformation. The spiritual darkness was dense, and though shafts of light had begun to penetrate, a great blaze of light was needed to effect any real and lasting change. The only source from which that light could come was the Scriptures.

The Reformation would have been impossible if God had not turned men back to the Bible to see in it the only authority for Christian doctrine and church order. Because the church had become so interwoven with the state and politics, it was inevitable that any reformation would come into conflict with politics. But the Reformation was not a political movement; it was a great movement of the Holy Spirit. Hence the basic principles which emerged in Reformation teaching were *sola Scriptura* (Scripture only), *sola gratia* (by grace alone) and *sola fide* (by faith alone).

Martin Luther

Luther was born on 10 November 1483. His parents were poor, but he was a young man of obvious ability and eventually he began studying to be a lawyer. His plans were dramatically altered in 1505 when he was nearly killed in a thunderstorm. In his anguish and fear he cried out, 'Help me, St Anne, and I will become a monk'.

❝ He came face to face with death, and he was not ready for it.

Martin Luther (1483-1546). A portrait of him by one of his friends, the artist Lucas Cranach.

He was terrified and convicted deeply, and he never forgot it. In a sense the Protestant Reformation starts with a thunderbolt! ❞
D.M. Lloyd-Jones

Luther survived the storm and kept his vow, entering the Augustinian monastery at Erfurt in Germany. He was a man of a very sensitive spirit, feeling deeply guilty for his sins and longing for peace with God. He followed all the prescribed remedies of the church — confessions, prayers, penance. He even went on a pilgrimage to Rome. But all to no avail — he knew no peace with God. Johann von Staupitz, the head of the Augustinian order in Germany, urged Luther to read the Bible. At first this only deepened his sense

of sin, and he spent years groping for the truth of God that would give his soul peace. During 1515 and 1516 he was lecturing to students on the Epistle to the Romans, and slowly the truth dawned on him that salvation comes by faith in what Christ has done for us.

❝ When the Holy Spirit revealed this to Luther, and he learned that it was by faith alone that he could be saved, and not by his own good works, the light of the truth shone with such brilliance, and brought such deliverance into his spirit, that he felt Paul's words, 'The just shall live by faith', were the very gate of Paradise itself. And so this great truth, THE JUST SHALL LIVE BY FAITH . . . became the fundamental truth of the Reformation. In other words, a wonderful reformation came personally to Luther before God used him as the instrument of the Reformation in Europe. ❞
S.M. Houghton

Luther's conversion not only brought him peace with God; it also brought him into conflict with the teaching of his church. This came to a head in 1517, when the pope was trying to raise money for the building of St Peter's Cathedral in Rome. One great fund-raiser was the sale of indulgences — that is, a certificate (to be bought only from the church) which guaranteed the purchaser, or a dead relative, a shorter time of punishment for sins in purgatory.

❝ This release from punishment is said to be possible because the church has a vast treasury of unused merits which have been accumulated primarily through the sufferings of Christ but also because of the good works of Mary and the saints who have done works more perfect than God's law requires for their own salvation. Thus not only the suffering and death of Christ, but also the good works of Mary and the saints, are the grounds of forgiveness of sins. The church claims to be able to withdraw merits from that store and to apply them to any member of the church just as if he had suffered what was necessary for the forgiveness of sins. ❞
L. Boettner

A monk named Tetzel was selling indulgences in Germany. He shamelessly exploited the fear and superstition of the people by declaring that *'no sooner will the money chink in the box, than the soul of the departed will be free'* from purgatory. At this point Luther still believed in indulgences, but he took great exception to this abuse. On 31 October 1517 he nailed to the door of the Castle Church in Wittenberg his famous Ninety-five Theses, which were copied, printed and distributed all over Germany. While the Theses attacked directly the abuse of indulgences, they also constituted an indirect attack on the pope himself, as witness Thesis 32:

❝ *Those who believe that they can be certain of their salvation because they have letters of indulgence will be eternally damned, together with their teachers.* **❞**

At first the pope dismissed the matter as a monk's squabble, but he soon changed his mind and demanded that Luther recant. Luther refused, and so on 15 June 1520 the pope excommunicated the reformer, ordering that his writings be burnt. Luther retaliated by burning publicly the pope's official order and other Catholic documents. The Reformation had begun.

The full might of Rome was

Luther burning the pope's bull. From the picture by F. Martersteig.

For example, when in 1521 he was called to meet his enemies in the city of Worms, his friends, remembering what had happened to Jan Hus, urged him not to go. His famous answer was, *'Though there were as many devils in Worms as tiles on its roofs, I would go.'* He did go, and in face of the demand that he recant and withdraw his writings he said:

❝ *Unless I am convinced by testimonies of the Scriptures or by clear arguments that I am in error — for popes and councils have often erred and contradicted themselves — I cannot withdraw, for I am subject to the Scriptures I have quoted; my conscience is captive to the Word of God. It is unsafe and dangerous to do anything against one's conscience. Here I stand; I cannot do otherwise. So help me God.* **❞**

On the way home from Worms Luther was 'kidnapped' by some friends and hidden for nearly a year in the castle of Wartburg. His enemies thought he was dead, so he was safe for a while. He spent that year in the study of the Bible and in translating the New Testament into German. The exile ended in March 1522 when Luther returned to Wittenberg. For the remaining twenty-four years of his life he devoted himself to preaching and writing. By 1534 he had translated the Old Testament, so now the whole Bible was available to the German people. This was important, because it ensured that the Reformation was

now thrown against Luther. But this papal power which had humbled emperors and burnt reformers found in the preacher of Wittenberg a far more difficult opponent. Luther was a man of remarkable courage and strength.

built, not on the word of Martin Luther, but on the Word of God.

Luther was a great man but not a perfect one. He made many mistakes in actions and doctrines, but he was instrumental in the hand of God in starting the Reformation. His own motives were expressed clearly when he appeared at Worms:

❝ *For it is not in a spirit of rashness, or with a view to personal advantage, that I have taught the doctrine with which I am reproached; I have done it in obedience to my conscience, and to the oath which, as doctor, I took to the Holy Scriptures; I have done it for the glory of God, the safety of the Christian Church, the good of the German nation, and the extirpation of many superstitions, abuses, and evils, disgrace, tyranny, blasphemy and impiety.* **❞**

Ulrich Zwingli

At the very time when Luther was reforming in Germany, a totally independent work was going on in Switzerland. Here, God's man was Ulrich Zwingli, who was born a year after Luther.

❝ *The Swiss took their stand strongly on the Word of God as the only rule of faith and practice, and were not bound by so many mediaeval traditions as the early Lutherans. They swept away images, relics, pictures, pilgrimages*

The Wartburg: the castle near Eisenach where Luther translated the New Testament into German.

and the use of the organ in public worship. Generally speaking, it may be said that the Reformation in Switzerland was very much more radical than in Germany. **"**
A.M. Renwick

In 1515 Zwingli began to preach in Zürich, and great crowds came to hear him.

" *Zwingli's faith was the same as Luther's, but more the result of reasoning. Luther advances with a bound. Zwingli owes more to clearness of perception. Luther's writings are pervaded with thorough personal conviction of the benefits which the cross of Christ confers upon himself, and this conviction, glowing with heat and life, is the soul of all he says. The same thing doubtless exists in Zwingli, but in an inferior degree. He had looked more to the Christian system as a whole, and admired it particularly for its beauty, for the light which it sheds into the human mind, and the eternal life which it brings to the world. The one is more the man of heart, the other more the man of intellect.* **"**
Merle d'Aubigné

Speaking of Luther, Zwingli said:

" *If Luther preaches Christ, he does what I do; those who have been brought to Christ by him are more numerous than those who have been brought by me. But no matter! I am not willing to bear any other name than that of Christ, whose soldier I am, and*

who alone is my head. Never was a single scrap written by me to Luther, or by Luther to me. And why? In order to show how well the Spirit of God accords with himself, since, without having heard each other, we harmoniously teach the doctrine of Jesus Christ.* **"**

Many parts of Switzerland accepted the Reformation doctrines and became Protestant, but others remained firmly Catholic. This division led ultimately to civil war when, in 1531, the Catholics raised an army of eight thousand men and invaded the Protestant centre of Zürich. Zwingli himself was killed in the battle. Thus, at the age of forty-seven, a great man of God died, and it seemed for a while as though the Reformation light had been extinguished in Switzerland.

John Calvin

" *Few men have suffered more from ignorant detraction than John Calvin. It would be well for some of those who condemn him out of hand to spend some little time studying his works. There is general agreement among serious scholars that Calvin was the greatest man of the Reformation era.* **"**
A.M. Renwick

John Calvin was born at Noyon in France on 10 July 1509. He studied law in Orléans, but in about 1532 he experienced what he described as a 'sudden conversion', the details of which are not

John Calvin (1509-1564). He is 27 years of age in this picture.

known. Soon he linked up with Protestants in Paris, but in 1533 he had to flee from that city because of his new biblical views. By 1535 he had settled as a refugee in the Swiss city of Basel, and the following year he published *The Institutes of the Christian Religion.* For a young man of twenty-six to have produced such a great work is truly amazing! Something of the greatness of this systematic exposition of biblical theology can be appreciated from the following opinions expressed by twentieth-century historians:

'Apart from the Bible itself, the most important book ever printed on the subject of the Christian faith' (S.M. Houghton).

'As a presentation of Christian doctrine it has never been surpassed' (A.M. Renwick).

'The most orderly and systematic popular presentation of doctrine and of the Christian life that the Reformation produced' (W. Walker).

Calvin's name is for ever linked with the Swiss city of Geneva. He planned originally to stay there only one night, but William Farel, another Frenchman already ministering in the city, prevailed on the reluctant Calvin to join him. Calvin's own account runs as follows:

◄

The Monument to the Reformers at Geneva.

66 *Farel, who burned with an extraordinary zeal to advance the gospel, immediately strained every nerve to detain me. And after he had learned that my heart was set upon devoting myself to private studies, and finding that entreaties were in vain, he went on to say that God would curse my retirement and the peace of study that I sought, if I withdrew and refused my help when the need for it was so urgent. I was so terror-stricken that I abandoned the journey I had planned; but I was so sensible of my natural shyness and timidity that I would not bind myself to accept any particular office.* **99**

The two Frenchmen began working together in Geneva in 1536. The city already had laws against such things as gambling, drunkenness and dancing, but they were not being observed. Calvin insisted that church members should not only keep such laws, but should live their lives in accordance with New Testament standards. The strict discipline that was introduced was unpopular with many, and on 23 April 1538 Calvin and Farel were banished from Geneva.

For the next three years Calvin lived in Strasbourg, where he was pastor of a French church. Meanwhile, there was a serious deterioration in the situation in Geneva and it was decided to invite Calvin to return. Again he was reluctant, but he finally consented and returned to Geneva, practically on his own terms, on 13 September 1541.

Under Calvin, Geneva became a refuge for persecuted Protestants from many lands. Here John Knox and a number of other Scottish and English Christians found safety. In fact, these refugees prepared a new English translation of the Bible there — the famous Geneva Bible published in 1560.

ᴄ *Calvin's influence extended far beyond Geneva. Thanks to his Institutes, his pattern of church government in Geneva, his academy, his commentaries, and his constant correspondence, he moulded the thought and inspired the ideals of the Protestantism of France, the Netherlands, Scotland, and the English Puritans. His influence penetrated Poland and Hungary, and before his death Calvinism was taking root in southwestern Germany itself. Men thought his thoughts after him. His was the only system that the Reformation produced that could organize itself powerfully in the face of governmental hostility, as in France and England. It trained strong men, confident in their election to be fellow workers with God in the accomplishment of His will, courageous to do battle, insistent on character, and confident that God has given in the Scriptures the guide of all right human conduct and proper worship. The spiritual disciples of Calvin, in most various lands, bore one common stamp. This was Calvin's work, a mastery of mind over mind, and certainly by the time of his death in Geneva, on May 27, 1564, he deserved the description of 'the only international reformer'.* **ᵑ**
W. Walker

Luther, Zwingli and Calvin were great men, but still fallible and with their own share of human weakness. They disagreed on some doctrines, and their actions on certain issues were far from satisfactory. In many ways they were men of their time, but even though some of their reforms did not go far enough, they were unquestionably men of the Scriptures. Consequently, under God, they were enabled to begin the work of turning the church back to its apostolic foundations.

The Reformation in England

At the beginning of the sixteenth century, despite the preaching of Wycliffe 150 years earlier, England was very much under the papal authority at Rome. To quote just one example of this, on 4 April 1519 a widow was burned alive in Coventry for the crime of teaching her children the Lord's Prayer and the Ten Commandments in English. King Henry VIII was himself a staunch Catholic who, as a reward for writing a treatise against Luther entitled *Assertion of the Seven Sacraments,* had received from the pope the title of 'Defender of the Faith'. In 1534 Henry broke with Rome because the pope would not annul his marriage to Catherine of Aragon and declared himself 'Supreme Head of the Church of England'. Yet even then he remained an ardent Catholic at heart and

King Henry VIII, after the painting by Holbein.

introduced scarcely any changes in the worship and ceremony of the church. Certainly, he was never a Protestant, nor did he ever have any sympathy with the Reformation. So the Reformation in England was not brought about because the king wanted a new wife. It was men like William Tyndale, Thomas Bilney, Hugh Latimer and Thomas Cranmer who were the instruments of a real and lasting reformation.

ENGLISH MONARCHS FROM 1485 TO THE PRESENT DAY

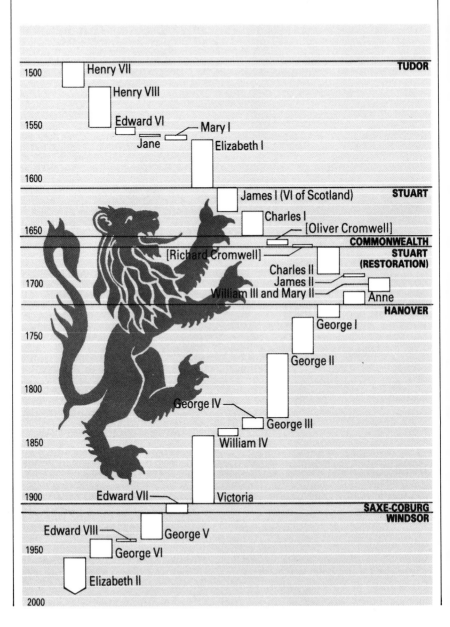

1500 — Henry VII — **TUDOR**
Henry VIII
1550 — Edward VI — Mary I
Jane
Elizabeth I
1600
James I (VI of Scotland) — **STUART**
Charles I
1650 — [Oliver Cromwell]
COMMONWEALTH
[Richard Cromwell] — **STUART (RESTORATION)**
Charles II
1700 — James II
William III and Mary II — Anne
HANOVER
George I
1750
George II
1800
George IV
George III
1850 — William IV
Edward VII — Victoria
1900
SAXE-COBURG
WINDSOR
Edward VIII — George V
1950 — George VI
Elizabeth II
2000

In 1525 William Tyndale completed the translation of the New Testament into English. For this he was hounded by the church, imprisoned and finally burnt in 1536. His one desire throughout his life had been that even the English plough-boy should know and understand the Scriptures. That desire was still dominant at his death, and his last words were, *'Lord, open the king of England's eyes.'*

Hugh Latimer received the degree of bachelor of theology in 1524, and his early attacks on the reformers caused him to be hailed as a great champion of the church who would refute their doctrines. One man thought otherwise. He was Thomas Bilney, who had been saved some time before through reading the New Testament and now had a great desire to see Latimer converted. But how could he get him to hear the gospel? He went to Latimer saying, *'For the love of God, be pleased to hear my confession'*, and Latimer, thinking that perhaps his own preaching had converted the heretic, gladly consented. Kneeling before Latimer, Bilney

❝ *related to him with touching simplicity the anguish he had once felt in his soul, the efforts he had made to remove it; their unprofitableness so long as he determined to follow the precepts of the church and, lastly, the peace he had felt when he believed that Jesus Christ is* the Lamb of God that taketh away the sin of the world. *He described to Latimer the*

William Tyndale (c.1494-1536).

spirit of adoption he had received, and the happiness he experienced in being able now to call God his Father. Latimer, who expected to receive a confession, listened without mistrust. His heart was opened, and the voice of the pious Bilney penetrated it without obstacle. From time to time the confessor would have chased away the new thoughts which came crowding into his bosom; but the penitent continued. His language, at once so simple and so lively, entered like a two-edged sword. Bilney was not without assistance in his work. A new, a strange witness — the Holy Ghost — was speaking in Latimer's soul. He learned from God to know God: he received a new heart. At length grace prevailed: the penitent rose up, but Latimer remained seated, absorbed in thought. The strong cross-bearer contended in vain

against the words of the feeble Bilney. Like Saul on the way to Damascus, he was conquered, and his conversion, like the apostle's, was instantaneous. **"**
Merle d'Aubigné

Latimer was the mighty preacher that England needed, and God used him greatly.

In 1547 Henry died and was succeeded by his son Edward VI. He was only ten years of age when he came to the throne and he died when he was sixteen. Edward, however, had been trained by Archbishop Cranmer and was a sincere supporter of the Reformation, which made great strides during his short reign. When Edward died, Mary Tudor became queen after a short power struggle. She was determined to restore Roman Catholicism in England, and so the Protestants faced severe persecution. Nearly 300 were burnt at the stake, including Latimer and Cranmer. On 30 November 1554 the pope was once again the head of the Church of England. Preaching was now banned and Roman Catholic ceremonies were restored. Under Mary's reign the Reformation would have been buried if it had merely consisted in passing laws and taking political decisions; but, because it was a matter of God striving with the hearts of men, not even the ferocity of Mary Tudor could destroy it.

In 1558, on the death of Mary, her half-sister Elizabeth came to the throne and the persecution ceased. Although Elizabeth had no

Thomas Cranmer (1489-1556), Archbishop of Canterbury.

strong sympathies with the Protestants, she was faced with a nation in turmoil and, for the sake of her own security on the throne, was obliged to move in their direction. A new Act of Supremacy in 1559 made her Supreme Governor of the Church of England. Many changes followed, including the demand that the clergy accept the Thirty-nine Articles of Religion, which was a clear statement of Reformed doctrine. Elizabeth, however, would not permit all the changes that the Protestants wanted. Her concern was to have a broad, national, comprehensive church; but she was facing men of deep religious convictions who wanted more thoroughgoing reforms. These men fell into two categories:

66 Cartwright and his fellow Puritans opposed all separation from the Church of England. Their thought was to introduce as much of Puritan discipline and practice as possible, and wait for

Mary Tudor, Queen of England: a portrait dated 1554 by Hans Eworth.

its further reformation by the government. Such a hope did not seem vain. Within a generation, the constitution and worship of the church of the land had been four times altered. Might it not soon be changed for a fifth time into what the Puritans deemed a more Scriptural model? They would

Elizabeth I: an effigy from her tomb in Westminster Abbey.

agitate and wait. This remained the program of the Puritans generally.

There were some, however, to whom this delay seemed unjustifiable. They would establish what they conceived to be Scriptural at once. These were the Separatists. **"**
W. Walker

The Puritans were remarkable and godly men, without whom the Reformation in England could have gone sadly astray.

The Reformation in Scotland

The Reformation in England made Scotland very important politically. The French virtually ruled the country, and Roman Catholic authority was supreme. It was therefore an ideal base from which to attack Protestant England.

There had been a few biblical preachers in Scotland, but little spiritual progress had been made. Then came John Knox, of whom it was said, *'Other men sawed the branches of the Papistry. This man lays his axe to the trunk of the tree.'* After several years in exile, Knox returned to Scotland in 1559, and by the time Mary Queen of Scots returned in 1561 the Reformation was firmly established.

Knox set Scotland firmly on the road of Presbyterianism. Like all the reformers, he had to face much opposition, but he was a strong and spiritual man. Spurgeon commented: *'When John Knox went upstairs to plead with God*

*for Scotland, it was the greatest
event in Scottish history.'*

The sixteenth century saw both
England and Scotland won for the
Reformation; but the struggle was
not over. The seventeenth century
brought its own problems in the
shape of the Stuart kings: James I,
Charles I, Charles II and James II.

Determined that he would make
the Puritans conform or else *'harry
them out of the land',* James I
demanded full compliance with the
Church of England pattern which
he had established. His demand
met with a direct refusal from 1,500
clergymen and added fuel to the
fire of the Separatists' cause.
English Puritanism now included
Presbyterians, Baptists and
Independents (later called
Congregationalists). In 1620, on
account of the persecution they
faced, a group of Independents set
sail from Plymouth for New
England. In the course of the next
twenty years these early 'Pilgrim
Fathers' were followed by 20,000
more men and women in search of
religious freedom. These were days
of great turmoil in the land. They
culminated in the Civil War
(1642-46), through which Oliver
Cromwell came to power and
sought to establish religious
liberty.

Three great declarations of faith
were drawn up by the Puritans in
the seventeenth century: the
Westminster Confession of Faith
(Presbyterian) of 1647, the Savoy

**John Knox (c.1514-1572): a statue of him
outside St Giles' Cathedral, Edinburgh.**

Declaration (Independent) of 1658, and the Baptist Confession of 1689. These confessions differed on matters such as baptism and church government, but on the essential doctrines of salvation they were all agreed.

The seventeenth century also witnessed the passing of severe Acts of Parliament against the Puritans. The Act of Uniformity of 1662 demanded that the Book of Common Prayer be used *'by all and every Minister or Curate in every Church, Chappell, or other place of Publique Worship within this Realm of England'*. Failure to comply led to removal from office, and thus nearly 2,000 ministers were driven from their churches. They were known as the 'Dissenters'.

This Act was followed by the Five Mile Act of 1665. Acknowledging that many had not complied with the Act of Uniformity, having *'taken upon themselves to preach in unlawful Assemblyes, Conventicles or Meetings'*, this Act forbade preachers to come within five miles of a city or town.

James II came to the throne in 1685. He determined to make England once again a Roman Catholic country. This aroused the opposition of both bishops and dissenters, and in 1688 he was forced to leave the country. His daughter Mary and her Dutch husband William of Orange were proclaimed joint sovereigns of England.

❝ *It was the beginning of a new epoch and made for lasting stability in Church and State. In England, the Anglican Church was approved as the established Church. The Toleration Act of 1689 alleviated the position of Nonconformists but inequalities continued for many years. In a short period they grew up so*

rapidly in numbers that one thousand new places of worship were built. By this time, three parties were distinguishable in the Anglican Church — High, Evangelical and Broad (or Latitudinarian). **"**
A.M. Renwick

A meeting of the Westminster Assembly. From a painting by J.R. Herbert. The Assembly met between 1643 and 1649. Its main work included the preparation of the Westminster Confession of Faith (1647).

8
Eighteenth-Century Revivals

Morally and spiritually England was in a sorry state at the beginning of the eighteenth century.

From almost every aspect of British life there arises evidence that an unwonted heartlessness had come over the nation. The Puritans had prohibited sports which indulged in cruelty to animals, but in the age of gin a traffic in games which found their pleasure in torturing beasts was carried on throughout the land, and the people had become so callous that they could look on suffering and delight in it.

*The generality of England's upper class manifested a deep-seated inhumanity . . . Far below them there existed the vast numbers of the poor. Of course, every country has its poor in every age, but, as England became more and more enfeebled by its long rejection of moral restraint and its indulgence in gin, larger and larger numbers of them became unable or unwilling to work.**
A. Dallimore

Such moral decadence is always the result of prior spiritual decay.

The rejection of the Puritans almost extinguished biblical Christianity in the nation. The ministers who had been forced by the Act of Uniformity to leave the church were replaced by men

" with little regard even to the decencies of the sacred office: the voluptuous, the indolent, the ignorant, and even the profane, *received episcopal orders, and like a swarm of locusts overspread the Church. "*
J.B. Marsten

The same was true of Wales. In 1721 Erasmus Saunders wrote *A*

The Holy Club, Oxford, with John Wesley addressing its members. George Whitefield is seated to the left of John Wesley.

View of the State of Religion in the Diocese of St. David's, in which he tells us:

❝ *So many of our churches are in actual ruins; so many more are ready to fall . . . roofs decaying, tottering and leaky, walls green, mouldy and nauseous.* **❞**

He goes on to comment on how few ministers were available, one curate being responsible for three or four churches ten miles or more apart:

❝ *Some men ordained were barely able to read and had no idea of being called by God to the work. They entered the ministry because they were not likely to succeed in any other profession.* **❞**

Such was the spiritual state of Wales. Yet, when Saunders penned these words in 1721, not far away from St. David's were two young boys, Howel Harris (aged seven) and Daniel Rowland (aged eight), through whom God was going to change the face of the nation. England too at this time could never have imagined the amazing changes that were to be effected through the mighty preaching of George Whitefield (born 1714) and John Wesley (born 1703).

—— England ——

In 1728 some students at Oxford University founded a society dubbed by unsympathetic onlookers 'The Holy Club'. Later, this small group of earnest and serious-minded men were nicknamed by their fellow students 'Methodists'. Charles Wesley was one of the founders, but soon after his brother John assumed the leadership. They were joined in 1733 by George Whitefield. These men sought to study the Bible, help the poor, visit the sick and those in prison; but though they did a great deal of good, none of them knew forgiveness of sin through the grace of God in the Lord Jesus Christ. Whitefield was converted in 1735, and the Wesley brothers in 1738. All three were ordained ministers of the Church of England. God now began to use these men in a most amazing way.

George Whitefield

George Whitefield was probably the greatest preacher that England had ever known.

❝ *His message was the Gospel of God's forgiving grace, and of peace through acceptance of Christ by faith, and a consequent life of joyful service. His few printed sermons give little sense of his power. Dramatic, pathetic, appealing, with a voice of marvellous expressiveness, the audiences of two continents were as wax melted before him.* **❞**
W. Walker

George Whitefield (1714-1770): a portrait by Nathaniel Hone.

His preaching shook the nation, and thousands flocked to hear him. His doctrine was evangelical and Calvinistic, and this aroused much opposition in the Church of England — so much so that many pulpits were barred to him. Whitefield then followed the example of the Welshman Howel Harris and began preaching in the open air.

*** Open-air preaching is now so commonplace that it is difficult to realize how outlandish it seemed then. There had long been propaganda to the effect that any display of spiritual earnestness might lead to trouble — even to civil disorder — and the generality of Englishmen believed it. Public opinion confined the clergyman to a narrow area of activity, and though this might include such things as drunkenness and gambling, it left no room for evangelistic fervour. ***
A. Dallimore

His first open-air sermon was to the miners at Kingswood in Bristol. He said afterwards:

*** Blessed be God that I have now broken the ice! I believe I never was more acceptable to my Master than when I was standing to teach those hearers in the open fields. Some may censure me; but if I thus pleased men, I should not be the servant of Christ. **99**

Crowds of over 20,000 began attending these services, and many were saved.

Whitefield's ministry lasted for thirty-five years, ranging all over England, Wales and Scotland, and including seven visits to America. He was blessed with great natural gifts of oratory, but this was not the reason for his success as a preacher. He was pre-eminently a spiritual, godly man. The phrases that abound in his *Journals* and letters give clear evidence of this. For example:

66 *'Night and day Jesus fills me with His love.'*
'The love of Christ strikes me quite dumb.'
'I walk continually in the comforts of the Holy Ghost.'
'The sight I have of God by faith ravishes my soul: how I shall be ravished when I see Him face to face.' **99**

C.H. Spurgeon said of him:

66 *Years on years, Whitefield continued his arduous labours, never resting. In the intervals of preaching, he was riding, or walking, and composing sermons. He wrote letters, conversed with enquirers, visited gaols and sick-beds, — attended to the Orphan House, published various works,*

preached during his voyages, — and at all times, even till the hour of death, was earnest and fervent . . . In his sermons one perceives coals of juniper and hot thunderbolts . . . He lived. Other men seem to be only half-alive; but Whitefield was all life, fire, wing, force. **99**

John Wesley

After leaving Oxford, John Wesley went as a missionary to Georgia. At this time he was still unconverted, and his work there was a failure. He returned to England in 1738 and on 24 May attended a meeting in Aldersgate Street, London. His brother Charles had been saved three days previously, and now, as John listened to the reading of Martin Luther's Preface to the Epistle to the Romans, he too came to saving faith in Christ. He wrote:

66 *I felt my heart strangely warmed. I felt I did trust in Christ, Christ alone, for salvation; and an assurance was given me, that He had taken away my sins, even mine, and saved me from the law of sin and death.* **99**

Wesley was a changed man, and his preaching also changed. As a result he, like Whitefield, found that pulpits were closed to him. It was no easy thing for him to follow Whitefield's example and preach in the open air. He recorded in his *Journal*:

John Wesley (1703-1791): a portrait of him at the age of 63.

*** I could scarce reconcile myself at first to this strange way of preaching in the fields . . . having been all my life (till very lately) so tenacious of every point relating to decency and order, that I should* have thought the saving of souls almost a sin if it had not been done in a church. **

*** One of the great features of eighteenth-century revivals was the abundance of great hymns they produced. Up to this point the churches had generally only sung psalms in worship. The new Christians wanted more expressions of praise and responded warmly to the hymns of Isaac Watts, Philip Doddridge, John Newton and Charles Wesley. **

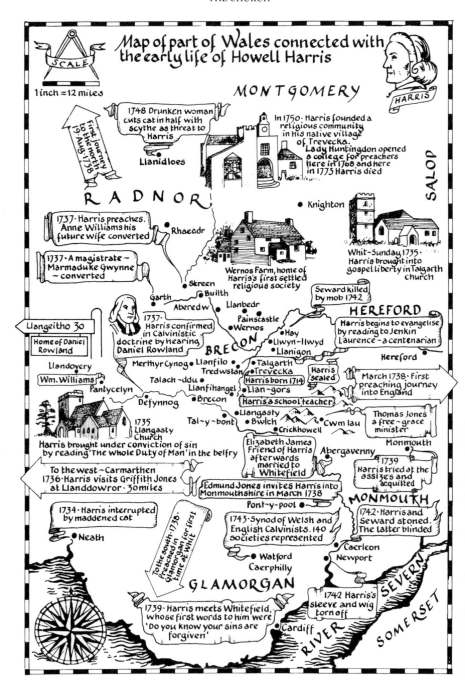

Map of part of Wales connected with the early life of Howell Harris

SCALE
1 inch = 12 miles

HARRIS

MONTGOMERY

SALOP

First journey to the north. 19. Aug. 1738

1748 Drunken woman cuts cat in half with scythe as threat to Harris

Llanidloes

In 1750. Harris founded a religious community in his native village of Trevecka. Lady Huntingdon opened a college for preachers here in 1768 and here in 1773 Harris died

RADNOR

Knighton

1737. Harris preaches. Anne Williams his future wife converted

Rhaeadr

1737. A magistrate ~ Marmaduke Gwynne ~ converted

Wernos Farm, home of Harris's first settled religious society

Whit~Sunday 1735. Harris brought into gospel liberty in Talgarth church

Skreen

Garth   Builth

Aberedw   Llanbedr

1737. Harris confirmed in Calvinistic doctrine by hearing Daniel Rowland

Painscastle
Wernos

Seward killed by mob 1742

HEREFORD

Harris begins to evangelise by reading to Jenkin Laurence ~ a centenarian

Llangeitho 30
Home of Daniel Rowland

BRECON

Hay
Llwyn~llwyd
Llanigon

Hereford

Llandovery
Wm. Williams
Pantycelyn

Merthyr Cynog   Llanfilo
Tredwstan   Talgarth
Trevecka

Talach~ddu

Harris born 1714

Harris 'sealed'

March 1738. First preaching journey into England

Llanfihangel   Llan~gors

Harris a school teacher

Defynnog   Brecon

1735
Llangasty
Church

Tal~y~bont

Llangasty
Bwlch

Crickhowell

Cwm Iau

Thomas Jones a free ~ grace minister

Harris brought under conviction of sin by reading 'The whole Duty of Man' in the belfry

Elizabeth James friend of Harris afterwards married to Whitefield

Abergavenny

Monmouth

To the west ~ Carmarthen 1736. Harris visits Griffith Jones at Llanddowror. 30 miles

Edmund Jones invites Harris into Monmouthshire in March 1738

1739
Harris tried at the assizes and acquitted

MONMOUTH

1734. Harris interrupted by maddened cat

Neath

To the south~1738. Morgan for first time at Whit. preached in Glamorgan

Pont~y~pool

1743. Synod of Welsh and English Calvinists. 140 societies represented

1742. Harris and Seward stoned. The latter blinded

Caerleon
Newport

Watford
Caerphilly

GLAMORGAN

1739. Harris meets Whitefield, whose first words to him were 'Do you know your sins are forgiven'

Cardiff

1742 Harris's sleeve and wig torn off

RIVER SEVERN

SOMERSET

But this reluctance was overcome, and so began a ministry that was to occupy the remainder of his life.

❝ *In fifty years he travelled 250,000 miles, mostly on horseback, during his evangelistic tours. Remarkable scenes were constantly witnessed as he preached the gospel. Hardened sinners could be seen at open-air meetings with tears of penitence rolling down their cheeks. The roughest in the land came humbly to the foot of the cross.* **❞**
A.M. Renwick

In doctrine, Whitefield was a Calvinist and Wesley an Arminian. This caused serious problems at times; but the Revival was a sovereign work of God, and what could have been a fatal hindrance was not allowed to be so.

—— Wales ——

Howel Harris

Howel Harris of Trefecca was born in the same year as Whitefield (1714) and was converted at the age of twenty-one. Immediately, he began witnessing to friends of the grace of God and sought to prepare himself to enter the ministry. He was never ordained by the Church of England but, contrary to church laws, he went about as a religious teacher — a practice which aroused much opposition from the clergy. Harris said about himself at this time:

❝ *A strong necessity was laid upon me, that I could not rest, but must go to the utmost of my ability to exhort. I could not meet or travel with anybody, rich or poor, young or old, without speaking to them concerning their souls. I went during the festive season from house to house in our parish, and the parishes of Llangors and Llangasty, until persecution became too hot. I was*

Howel Harris (1714-1773).

absolutely dark and ignorant with regard to the reasons of religion: I was drawn onwards by the love I had experienced, as a blind man is led, and therefore I could not take notice of anything in my way . . .
At first I knew nothing at all,

but God opened my mouth (full of ignorance), filling it with terrors and threatenings. I was given a commission to rend and break sinners in the most dreadful manner. I thundered greatly, denouncing the gentry, the carnal clergy and everybody. **"**

In a land that was dark with sin and ignorance, Harris was God's man. He was a great preacher or, as he called himself, an exhorter, and hundreds were converted through his ministry. This great movement of the Holy Spirit in Wales was for a number of years independent of the work in England, and had in fact begun two years earlier.

Harris had exceptional gifts of organization, and he set up 'societies' for the new converts.

Wernos, a farmhouse near Builth Wells in Powys, was the meeting-place of the first permanent society for believers in Wales.

" *The object of the societies was primarily to provide a fellowship in which the new spiritual life and experience of the people could be safeguarded and developed. The great emphasis was primarily on experience and the experimental knowledge of God and His love and His ways. Each member gave an account of God's dealings with him or her, and reported on any remarkable experience, and also their sins and lapses, and so doing compared notes with one another in these respects. The societies were not 'bible study' groups or meetings for the discussion of theology. Of course great stress was laid on reading the Bible as well as prayer, but the more intellectual aspects of the Faith were dealt with in the preaching services and not in the societies. Here, the emphasis was on daily life and living, the fight against the world, the flesh and the devil, and the problems that arise inevitably in the Christian's pilgrimage through this world of sin.* **"**
D.M. Lloyd-Jones

By any standards, Howel Harris was a remarkable man. He was preaching in the open air long before Whitefield, and he was organizing societies, which became one of the great features of Wesleyan Methodism, two years before Wesley was converted.

William Williams

Another leader of the Revival in Wales was William Williams of Pantycelyn. He is best known today for his hymns; but he was also a preacher, and particularly a leader of society meetings. Dr Lloyd-Jones said of him:

William Williams, Pantycelyn (1717-1791).

66 *His genius, his spiritual understanding, and what would now be described as psychological insight stand out everywhere and are truly astonishing.* **99**

Daniel Rowland

Thirdly, we must single out Daniel Rowland. Rowland was minister of the church at Llangeitho, but unconverted. Upon his conversion (at about the same time as Howel Harris) there was a great change in his preaching. The wrath of God and the eternal consequences of divine judgment were proclaimed powerfully and savingly. Thousands of people flocked to

Llangeitho to hear him. George Whitefield said:

66 *The power of God at the sacrament under the ministry of Mr Rowlands was enough to make a person's heart to burn within him. At seven of the morning have I seen perhaps ten thousand from different parts, in the midst of the sermon, crying* 'Gogoniant — Bendigedig' *[Glory — Blessed be God], ready to leap for joy. Such was his celebrity at this early time, that at seven o'clock in the morning so large a number assembled to hear him.* **99**

Rowland's preaching was not all about judgment. Indeed, after

Daniel Rowland (1713-1790).

hearing him, Thomas Charles of Bala, another great preacher of the day, wrote:

> **❝** *I had such a view of Christ as our High Priest, of His love, compassion, power, and all-sufficiency, as filled my soul with astonishment, with joy unspeakable and full of glory. My mind was overwhelmed and overpowered with amazement. The truths exhibited to my view appeared too wonderfully gracious to be believed. I could not believe for very joy. The glorious scenes then opened to my eyes will abundantly satisfy my soul millions of years hence in the contemplation of them. I had some idea of gospel truths before floating in my head, but they never powerfully and with divine energy, penetrated my heart till now.* **❞**

The leaders of the Revival in Wales were very distinctly Calvinistic in their doctrines, and Whitefield felt one with them. The Methodism that grew up in Wales, therefore, was Calvinistic Methodism. It combined the passion of the Methodists with the solid doctrinal base of Calvinism.

—— Scotland ——

The first signs of revival in Scotland appeared in the eighteenth century under the preaching of Ebenezer and Ralph Erskine. Their churches became crowded and, like Whitefield and Harris, they resorted to open-air preaching. Letters from the Erskines to Whitefield tell of Ebenezer preaching to 14,000 people and Ralph conducting a communion service with four or five thousand communicants.

In 1742, Cambuslang (near

Jonathan Edwards (1703-1758).

The eighteenth century witnessed remarkable movements of the Holy Spirit in revival, both in Britain and in the new colonies of North America under men like Jonathan Edwards.

❝ In the experience of the Church the eighteenth century was one continuous flow of revivals, which the Holy Spirit moulded from its infinite variety of situations, circumstances, impossibilities, instruments, and conditions, into one great healing stream. The leading revivalists were 'men of like passions as we are', subject to errors, sins and temptations, but the Holy Spirit used them in spite of their limitations and failings. As they preached, the Holy Spirit accompanied the Word with power and it became the 'savour of life' unto many. The deadness and barrenness which had prevailed in the Church, and the indifference and immorality which had abounded in the world, could not withstand the surge of spiritual life which flowed through mere men, but issued from a divine source. Whole communities were affected and transformed, great churches were reformed and invigorated, vast countries took on a new aspect. From this movement of God's Spirit new missionary enterprises were born, philanthropic institutions blossomed forth, and ecclesiastical foundations were consolidated. The repercussions of the movement not only traversed continents but also periods and ages, giving cause for generations to come to praise God, and securing for them a goodly heritage.❞
Eifion Evans

101

2 That they begin their meeting with prayer, by one of their Number.

3. That where it can be conveniently done, a part of a psalm be sung to the praise of God, according to the practise of Christ Mat. 26. 30. it being also an especial mean of Christian instruction. Coloss. 3. 16.

4 Then let one pray.

5 Then let them read a portion of the Lords word, at least one Chapter beginning at the new Testament.

6. After reading let another pray.

7 After this let one of the Society ask three or four questions out of Vincents Catechism, which the Society are to be advertised of at their former Meeting to prepare to answer.

8. Upon the back of this, One of their Number having prayed, if any present desire the advice of the Meeting anent their own spiritual state or anent what may be sin or duty in any particular concerning them, let it be kindly given, also if the Society observe any thing exceptionable in any member, let them admonish the member thereof in tenderness and love. It being the Duty of all Christians to take the oversight one of another. Heb. 12. 15. and to exhort one another. Heb. 3. 14.

9 Let no curious questions be proposed, that are either above the capacity of the Society or do not tend immediatly to the edifie ment of practical Religion, — These Paull, in many places of his Epistles to Timothy & Titus, warns to beware of.

10. It would also be helpfull in the way of duty to confer either now or at any other time during the meeting anent the sins of the Congregation in general, or of these places in particular within the bounds of the meeting that they may be bewailed & mourned over before the Lord and to warn one another agst them. this is warranted by the practise of the Godly, and the kind Notice the Lord takes of their doing so Mal. 3. 16.

11. That no member talk abroad any thing spoken or done in the Society.

12. That absent members give an account of the reason of their absence, which if not sustained, are to submitt them-

Rules for the prayer societies drawn up by the Kirk Session at Kilsyth, Scotland. Kilsyth, like Cambuslang, was a centre of revival in 1742.
◀

Glasgow) was the scene of a great revival under the ministry of William M'Culloch.

❝ *On Thursday, February 18, after several days in which a spirit of prayer had been especially evident, some fifty people detained their minister through the night as they sought spiritual help and relief from conviction of sin. From this point onwards the influence and success which followed the ministry of the Word was such that preaching now became M'Culloch's daily work. The whole parish with its nine hundred inhabitants was profoundly moved as quarrels, swearing, drunkenness, and all the other characteristics of worldliness gave way visibly to confession of wrongs, restitution, remorse and prayerfulness. 'The report', says a contemporary, 'spread like fire; vast multitudes were attracted thither. I believe that, in less than two months from its commencement, there were few parishes within twelve miles that had not more or less of their people awakened by resorting thither; and many who were awakened there came from places greatly more distant.'* **❞**
Iain Murray

Whitefield visited Cambuslang and wrote:

❝ *The awakening here in Scotland is unspeakable . . . God seems to awaken scores together. I never was enabled to preach so before.* **❞**

William M'Culloch himself said of this revival:

❝ *It is not quite five months since the work began, and during that time, I have reason to believe that upwards of five hundred souls have been awakened, brought under deep convictions of sin, and a feeling sense of their lost condition. Most of these have also, I trust, been savingly brought home to God.*

I do not include this in this number such as have been found to be mere pretenders, nor such as have had nothing in their exercise beyond a dread of hell . . .

I do not include in this number, either, such as have been awakened by Mr. Whitefield's sermons; because I cannot pretend to compute them. **❞**

9

The Nineteenth and Twentieth Centuries

A lifeless, formal Christianity will never have any concern or vision to evangelize the world; but when the church is invigorated by the fire of revival its outlook is transformed. It is not surprising, then, that the eighteenth-century revivals were followed in the nineteenth century by a period of great missionary expansion.

Missionaries

In 1792 twelve Baptist ministers in Northamptonshire formed the Baptist Missionary Society. In the following year the BMS sent out William Carey to work in India. Not all Christians were sympathetic to Carey. At a ministers' meeting which was held before he set out for India, Carey had urged his fellow ministers to be concerned for missions. An older minister had rebuked him, saying, *'Sit down, young man, and respect the opinion of your seniors. If the Lord wants to convert the heathen, He can do it without your help'*. Fortunately, Carey was not put off by such advice. His motto was, *'Expect great things from God; attempt great things for God'*. It was in

William Carey (1761-1834).

this spirit that he arrived at Calcutta in 1793. The work was hard and discouraging at first, but Carey remained in India until his death in 1834. He was followed by many other missionaries to India and other lands: for example, Henry Martyn (India), Adoniram Judson (Burma), David Livingstone (Africa), Robert

Morrison (China), John Williams and John Paton (Pacific Islands), and Hudson Taylor (China).

Social reformers

While missionaries were seeking to meet the deep spiritual needs in heathen lands, Christians at home were attempting to bring a Christian influence to bear on the social conditions of England. A group of evangelical Anglicans known as the 'Clapham Sect' were prominent in this sphere.

David Livingstone (1813-1873).

❝ *It was largely through their help and their enthusiasm that the agitation for the abolition of the slave-trade was successful. Zachary Macaulay had seen the evils of it while managing an estate in Jamaica. From 1787 onwards they kept the matter before Parliament. William Wilberforce took up the question with untiring energy and finally persuaded William Pitt to promote a Bill for the total abolition of the slave trade in 1807. In 1833 all slaves in British territory were emancipated. Members of the group, with the object of showing how the negroes ought to be treated, had already founded the Colony of Sierra Leone of which Zachary Macaulay was governor for seven years.* **❞**
A.M. Renwick

Later in the nineteenth century another evangelical Anglican, the Earl of Shaftesbury, worked strenuously to bring about social and industrial reforms. His record of success was amazing, including the securing of legislation to

Antony Ashley Cooper (1801-1885), seventh Earl of Shaftesbury.

" Great Britain was the first of the countries of the world to be industrialized, and its workers were caught in a treadmill of competitive drudgery which kept them straining full sixteen hours a day. Evangelical leaders, including Shaftesbury and members of the Clapham Sect, brought about an end to much of the sorry exploitation and promoted all sorts of social improvements. No less an authority than Prime Minister Lloyd George credited to the Evangelical Revival the movement which improved the condition of the working classes in wages, hours of labour and otherwise. "

J. Edwin Orr

prevent boy sweeps from being employed to climb up chimneys, and children under ten from having to work in the mines.

Revival

Revival came again to the church in 1859. It started in America in 1857, then spread to Ulster and Wales, Scotland and England. A million new members were added to the churches through this work of the Holy Spirit, and some of the individuals concerned in this revival were to be greatly used by God. D.L. Moody was converted in America in 1857 and became a great evangelist; while in Britain Thomas Barnardo was converted in 1862 and established his famous

◀

All Saints Church, Llangorwen, Dyfed. This church, which is near Aberystwyth, had close links with some of the leaders of the Oxford Movement. Isaac Williams supplied the finance for it to be built in 1841. J.Henry Newman provided a candelabra and John Keble contributed a lectern.

orphanages. Other significant developments in this period were the establishment of the Salvation Army, the YMCA, the Keswick Convention and the Brethren Assemblies.

Oxford Movement

But while the nineteenth century produced much that was good, it also witnessed the growth of anti-biblical influences within the church. One of these was the 'Oxford Movement' in the Church of England.

" Certain Oxford scholars . . . wished to turn back the Church to the type of churchmanship which prevailed before the 16th Century Reformation, and accordingly they set themselves to prove that the Church's 39 Articles really bore a different interpretation from that which evangelicals placed upon them, a claim not difficult to disprove. In other words, the movement veered towards Roman

Catholicism, and ultimately some of the leaders went over to that Church. **99**
S.M. Houghton

The Oxford Movement afflicted primarily the Church of England, and its influence can still be seen in that Church. But another anti-biblical phenomenon of the nineteenth century was to affect the Christian church as a whole. This was theological liberalism.

Liberalism
In 1859 Charles Darwin published his book *The Origin of Species.* The theory of evolution which it proposed not only contradicted the teaching of the first chapter of

Charles Robert Darwin (1809-1882).

Genesis but also, by implication, denied the Fall of man and the whole New Testament doctrine of salvation. Liberal theologians used evolutionary ideas in their approach to the Scriptures — an approach which denied their inspiration, denied the historicity of much of the biblical narrative and denied the miraculous. They taught that the Bible was not to be trusted and that Jesus Himself made mistakes.

They often claimed that science

Amsterdam: venue for the 1948 inaugural assembly of the World Council of Churches. ▶

was on their side. This gave even their most irresponsible claims an air of authority and authenticity. Liberalism made rapid progress in the churches, and few offered any effective opposition. One of the few was the Baptist minister Charles H. Spurgeon. In what became known as the 'Downgrade Controversy', he vigorously protested at the decline of biblical beliefs among some Baptist preachers. But Spurgeon received very little support, and he subsequently withdrew from the Baptist Union.

The Ecumenical Movement

The rejection by the churches of biblical truth and authority in the nineteenth century paved the way for the twentieth-century Ecumenical Movement. Without theological liberalism there could never have been an Ecumenical Movement. (The term 'ecumenical' comes from a Greek word meaning 'the whole inhabited world'.) The movement began in Edinburgh in 1910, when a number of missionary and church leaders gathered in conference. It was there that the concern for church unity was born, and in 1948, in Amsterdam, the World Council of Churches (or WCC for short) came into being. The WCC was defined at Amsterdam as 'a fellowship of churches which accept our Lord Jesus Christ as God and Saviour', but at the same time it was pointed out that this was 'not a credal test to judge churches or persons'. In other words, the Ecumenical Movement has no theological

basis; biblical truth is unimportant. Such an approach has proved very popular, and numerically the WCC is very strong; yet many would agree with the words of Dr Lloyd-Jones:

" *The starting point in considering the question of unity must always be regeneration and belief in the truth. Nothing else produces unity . . . it is impossible apart from this.* **"**

All Christians long for a true spiritual unity, but many do not see the World Council of Churches as helpful in achieving this. Speaking of the WCC, Roland Lamb, former Secretary of the British Evangelical Council, said:

" *Because of its plausible and inadequate basis of faith it has become so comprehensive that its member denominations inevitably disagree on what the gospel is. Hence it has more and more become preoccupied with social, political and humanitarian issues, to an almost total neglect of the church's evangelistic and missionary task.* **"**

Liberalism and ecumenism have made the twentieth century a difficult time for biblical Christianity, and the effect is seen in the huge decline in church attendance. At the beginning of the century about eighty-five per cent of the population went to church regularly in Britain: now the figure is about five per cent.

❝ *The greatest need of the hour is a new baptism and outpouring of the Holy Spirit in renewal and revival. Nothing else throughout the centuries has ever given the Church true authority and made her, and her message, mighty. But what right have we to pray for this, or to expect that He will honour or bless anything but the truth that He Himself enabled the authors of the Old Testament and New Testament to write? To ask Him to do so is not only near blasphemy but also the height of folly. Reformation and revival go together and cannot be separated. He is the 'Spirit of Truth', and He will honour nothing but the truth. The ultimate question facing us these days is whether our faith is in men and their power to organize, or in the truth of God in Christ Jesus and the power of the Holy Spirit. Let me put it another way. Are we primarily concerned about the size of the Church, or the purity of the Church, both in doctrine and in life? Indeed, finally it comes to this. Is our view of the Church Roman Catholic (inclusivist, organizational, institutional, and hierarchical) or Reformed, emphasizing the universal priesthood of all believers and the need for keeping the Church herself constantly under the judgment of the Word?* **❞**
D.M. Lloyd-Jones

Recommended Books

A History of the Christian Church: Williston Walker (T. & T. Clark)
The Story of the Church: A.M. Renwick (Inter-Varsity Press)
Sketches from Church History: S.M. Houghton (Banner of Truth)
From Christ to Constantine: M.A. Smith (Inter-Varsity Press)
The Church Under Siege: M.A. Smith (Inter-Varsity Press)
The Reformation in England, Vols. 1 & 2: J.H. Merle d'Aubigné (Banner of Truth).
George Whitefield, Vols. 1 & 2: Arnold Dallimore (Banner of Truth)

PART THREE
THE FAITH

To know *what* we believe, and *why* we believe
it, ought to be of prime importance to every
Christian. The following pages are written to give the
new believer an understanding of the basic doctrines
of the Christian faith.

Some Christians are afraid of doctrine; they seem
to think it is something hard and unprofitable. This is
sad, because all that doctrine seeks to do is to give
clear expression to what we believe. If Christians
avoid this, they not only impoverish their own
spiritual lives, but also make themselves less effective
as witnesses to the saving grace of the Lord Jesus
Christ.

Our only authority for belief and faith is the Bible,
so whenever a Bible reference is given, be sure to look
it up.

10
God

While it is true that man is incurably religious, and will therefore always create gods to worship, it is also true that, left to himself, man can never know the true and living God. Whether it is the sun, moon, stars, man-made idols of other civilizations, or the more sophisticated gods of our day such as self, pride, ambition or possessions, man must and will worship something. By so doing he exposes his ignorance of the true God. Indeed, even when people today attempt to worship the God and Father of our Lord Jesus Christ, all too often they fail to realize His greatness.

❝ The 'god' of this twentieth century no more resembles the Supreme Sovereign of Holy Writ than does the dim flickering of a candle the glory of the midday sun. ❞
A.W. Pink

The reason for this was well expressed by Martin Luther when he said, *'Your thoughts of God are too human'*. In other words, we tend to think of God merely as a reflection of ourselves. God complains of this in Psalm 50:21

— *'You thought I was altogether like you'*. But He is not like us, and the answer to the question 'What is God like?' is that He is not like anyone or anything (Isaiah 40:25; 46:5; Psalm 89:6-8).

God is gloriously and wondrously unique. Before the world was created, God existed. In fact, there never was a time when God did not exist, and if there had been no God, there would have been no world (Psalm 90:2). It is difficult for us to grasp such concepts, but that is only because, as Luther said, we think of God in a human way. There is only one way to escape this snare, and that is to centre our thoughts upon what God has chosen to reveal to us about Himself in the Scriptures. For the person who seriously wants to know God, and has many questions to ask, God has provided answers. They may not be the answers we expect; but they are God's answers, and they are to be found in His revealed Word.

In the Bible we discover the *attributes* of God.

❝ An attribute of God is whatever God has in any way

revealed as being true of Himself. **"**
A.W. Tozer

We need to know these things, because the study of God is the highest and greatest subject that can occupy the mind of a Christian. It is the most stimulating, most exciting, most satisfying and most comforting study possible.

Providence

By the providence of God we mean the unceasing activity of God the Creator working in the affairs of His creatures. He upholds, guides and governs all events and circumstances. Providence is presented in Scripture as the direct result of divine sovereignty. God is King over all, and He does what He wills. This is taught in both the Old Testament (Psalm 103:19) and the New (Ephesians 1:11).

" *Nothing will so enlarge the intellect, nothing so magnify the whole soul of man, as a devout, earnest, continued investigation of the great subject of the Deity. Would you lose your sorrow? Would you drown your cares? Then go, plunge yourself in the Godhead's deepest sea; be lost in his immensity; and you shall come forth as from a couch of rest, refreshed and invigorated. I know nothing which can so comfort the soul; so calm the swelling billows of sorrow and grief; so speak peace to the winds of trial, as a devout musing upon the subject of the Godhead.* **"**

C.H. Spurgeon

So let us consider some of the attributes of God.

Sovereignty

This means the absolute rule and authority of God over His creation. It is a rule that governs everything without exception — creation, animals, weather, and man's salvation. God is sovereign because He is God, and because He is supreme. The God of Scripture is no fairy-tale king, but the sovereign Lord, the King of kings (Job 23:13; 1 Chronicles 29:11-12; 2 Chronicles 20:6).

Holiness

Holiness is the attribute of God which Scripture emphasizes more than any other. It touches every other attribute. Thus God's justice is a holy justice, His love is a holy love, His wrath a holy wrath (Psalm 99:9; 111:9; Revelation 15:4). Holiness implies two things: complete freedom from all moral evil, and absolute moral perfection.

This is our God. He is holy. Holiness is the very beauty of God.

Immutability

This means that God never changes (Malachi 3:6; James 1:17). God's nature is such that He cannot change, because all change must be for the better or the worse. God cannot change for the better, because He is already perfect; and because He is perfect, He cannot change for the worse.

Goodness

Of this attribute Thomas Manton said:

❝ *He is originally good, good of Himself, which nothing else is; for all creatures are good only by participation and communication from God. He is essentially good; not only good, but goodness itself: the creature's good is a superadded quality, in God it is His essence. He is infinitely good; the creature's good is but a drop, but in God there is an infinite ocean or gathering together of good. He is eternally and immutably good, for He cannot be less good than He is; as there can be no addition made to Him, so no subtraction from Him.* **❞**

Omnipotence

God has all power (Isaiah 40:10ff).

Omniscience

God has all knowledge (Psalm 139:1-4).

Omnipresence

God is in all places (Psalm 139:7-8).

We could go on to think of the patience of God, and of His wisdom, love, grace and mercy. As Frederick Faber the hymn-writer puts it, He is 'God of a thousand attributes'.

My God, how wonderful Thou art,
Thy majesty how bright!
How beautiful Thy mercy-seat,
In depths of burning light!

The Great Nebula in Orion.

How wonderful, how beautiful,
The sight of Thee must be,
Thine endless wisdom, boundless
power,
And aweful purity!
F.W. Faber

11
Jesus

Jesus was not just a good man, a healer, teacher and prophet. He was all these things, but much more besides. The New Testament leaves us in no doubt as to who Jesus is:

He is the image of the invisible God, the firstborn over all creation. For by him all things were created.
Colossians 1:15,16

For in Christ all the fulness of the Deity lives in bodily form.
Colossians 2:9

The Son is the radiance of God's glory and the exact representation of his being.
Hebrews 1:3

Sunrise over Galilee.

In the Old Testament the prophet Isaiah was given a remarkable revelation of the glory and holiness of God. He sees and hears the angelic host crying:

❝ *Holy, holy, holy is the Lord Almighty; the whole earth is full of his glory.* **❞**
Isaiah 6:3

Isaiah himself says of this: *'My eyes have seen the King, the Lord Almighty'* (verse 5).

But in the New Testament, referring to this incident, the apostle John says: *'Isaiah said this because he saw Jesus' glory and spoke about him'* (John 12:41).

Jesus, then, is the holy God of whom the angels spoke. Jesus is the King, the Lord Almighty, whom Isaiah saw. Jesus is God.

His birth

The word used to describe the birth of Jesus is 'incarnation'. You will not find this word in the Bible. It comes from a Latin word meaning 'in the flesh', and it expresses the amazing truth that when Jesus was born, God became man (John 1:1,14). The Holy One identified Himself with sinful man and took our nature upon Himself. The hymn-writer Charles Wesley described the incarnation as
Our God contracted to a span, Incomprehensibly made man.

Jesus therefore had two natures: He was truly God and truly Man. This is a very difficult concept, but one that the Bible clearly teaches. Consider, for example, the following:

☐ Jesus is God (Philippians 2:5-11; Colossians 1:15-19; Hebrews 1:1-3).
☐ Jesus is Man (John 8:40; Acts 2:22; Hebrews 2:14-18).

The birth of Jesus was very special. The Old Testament prophet Isaiah and the New Testament writers Matthew and Luke all tell us that His mother Mary was a virgin. His birth was not the result of human love or lust, but came about through the remarkable life-giving operation of the Holy Spirit (Matthew 1:20; Luke 1:35). This may be baffling to our minds, but it is crucial to our salvation. If Jesus had been born as the result of a normal sexual relationship between man and woman, He would have been like all men, a sinner by nature, helpless to save Himself, let alone anyone else. But Jesus did not inherit a sinful nature, and His life of obedience to the law of God kept His nature sinless and pure. During His life He was *'tempted in every way, just as we are - yet was without sin'* (Hebrews 4:15).

His life

Why is the doctrine of the virgin birth crucial to our salvation? The reason Jesus came was to make atonement for our sin, and that meant that He had to die in our place, for death was the penalty God had decreed for sin. He came therefore to die as a sacrifice for us, in accordance with God's plan (Isaiah 53:5). But in order to do this, Jesus had to be *sinless,* so that death should have no rightful claims on Him. The slightest sin in Jesus would have made Him no different from all other men, and would have been sufficient to bring upon Him the penalty of death. In that case, there would have been no way in which He could have offered to die instead of us, because He would have had to die for His own sin. But, thank God, only hours before He was crucified, He was able to say, *'the prince of this world [that is, the devil] is coming. He has no hold on me'* (John 14:30). The sinlessness of the Saviour deprived the devil of any authority or control over Him. More than that, it made it impossible for the Evil One to make any legitimate demands upon Almighty God that the Lord Jesus Christ should die for His own sins.

The slopes of Mount Hermon. Some commentators have suggested that this mountain was the scene of the transfiguration of Jesus, i.e. the place where He revealed something of His glory to His disciples (see Mark 9:2-9).

The uniqueness of Jesus:
□ *He lived a unique life (Hebrews 4:15).*
□ *He exercises a unique authority (Matthew 7:29; 28:18).*
□ *He has a unique power (Matthew 24:30).*

Jesus is the fulfilment of all the Old Testament prophecies about the coming Messiah. As William Hendriksen reminds us:

" *There are 332 distinct prophecies in the Old Testament which have been literally fulfilled in Christ . . . the mathematical probability of all these prophecies being fulfilled in one man is represented by the fraction*

$$\frac{1}{840000000000000000000000000000000000000000000000}$$

*(97 noughts in all)***"**

His death and resurrection
We shall deal with the death of Jesus later; but we need to note here that, because of who He was, death could not hold Him (Acts 2:24). Jesus said He would rise from the dead, and He did. His rising from the grave was a literal, physical and bodily resurrection (Luke 24:37-39).

The resurrection of Jesus is
□ *crucial to our faith (1 Corinthians 15:12-19);*
□ *a guarantee of our resurrection (John 11:25; 1 Corinthians 15:20-23);*
□ *a confirmation of who He is (Romans 1:4).*

12
The Holy Spirit

The Holy Spirit is not merely a power or an influence; He is a Person (not 'it', but 'He'). It is easy to think of Jesus as a Person because He had a physical body as we do, but the Holy Spirit is not like this. Nevertheless, though He does not have a body like a person, the Scriptures speak of the Holy Spirit as having all the qualities of a person. For instance, He teaches (John 14:26), testifies (John 15:26), convicts (John 16:8), guides (John 16:13). These are the actions of a person, not of a mere power or influence. The personality of the Holy Spirit is so real that He can be grieved (Ephesians 4:30) and lied to (Acts 5:3).

His deity

It is important that we grasp this fact of the personality of the Holy Spirit, because the Holy Spirit is God. He is not just the power of God, an impersonal force at work in the world; but as the Father is

" In thinking about God the Holy Spirit, we must never lose sight of the fact that we are thinking about God. In some respects it may seem a little easier to conceive of God the Father, and also of the Lord Jesus Christ; but it is not quite so easy to think of God the Holy Spirit. It will become a little easier if we dismiss from our minds all ideas of bodily form when we think of God. The necessary thing for us to think is not what kind of outward appearance we can imagine Him to have, but what kind of will and character He has. The character of God has been very clearly revealed to us in all His actions. It is in this way, therefore, that it will perhaps become less difficult for us to think about the Holy Spirit. "

E.F. Kevan

God, and the Son is God, so too the Spirit is God.

We have already referred to Isaiah 6, and shown that *'the King, the Lord Almighty'* (verse 5) whom the prophet saw there was none other than the Lord Jesus (John 12:41). If you now turn to Acts 28:25-27, you will find Paul quoting from Isaiah 6, and he says that the Person who was speaking was the Holy Spirit. Just as Jesus is God, so also the Holy Spirit is God. There are many other verses in the Bible which speak of the Holy Spirit as possessing those qualities which belong to God alone (for example, Job 33:4; Psalm 139:7; Romans 15:19).

Fire is one of the symbols of the Holy Spirit (Matt.3:11; cf.Acts 2:3).

66 So the Holy Spirit is called God. He has the attributes of God. He does the works of God. He is invoked and honoured as God. We can only conclude that He is God, and that He is God in the same sense as are the Father and the Son. 99
Stuart Olyott

His ministry
The ministry and work of the Holy Spirit are essential to salvation. This is because salvation is exclusively the work of God. It has to be, because of what we are by nature. Jesus said we must be born again of the Holy Spirit because only *'the Spirit gives birth to spirit'* — that is, to a new spirit that is willing to serve God (John 3:6). Only the Holy Spirit can produce a *spiritual* change in man. Other agencies may change him for the better or for the worse: his life may be greatly enriched through discovering the joys of music, or it may be ruined by alcohol. But none of these changes affect what a man is before a holy God. He is born a sinner, and whether he becomes a cultured sinner or a drunken sinner, he is still a sinner. To alter a man's standing before God, a spiritual change is needed. This is the work of the Holy Spirit, and Jesus calls the beginning of this change being *'born again'*.

The first work of the Holy Spirit of which a man is personally aware is conviction of sin (read John 16:8-11). This conviction of our own sin, of Christ's righteousness, and of God's judgment, is necessary for salvation, and only the Holy Spirit can produce it.

When we become Christians, the ministry of the Holy Spirit spreads throughout our lives and enriches them by making the things of God and the Person of Jesus more real and precious to us (John 16:12-15). There are so many things that God wants us to know and experience:

❝ *No eye has seen, no ear has heard, no mind has conceived what God has prepared for those who love him.* **❞**
1 Corinthians 2:9.

This verse is speaking not of heaven, but of blessings that can be experienced in this world, here and now — but only as God reveals them to us by His Spirit (verse 10).

The Christian is indwelt by the Holy Spirit (Romans 8:9), and one of the great benefits of this is assurance of salvation (Romans 8:14-17). Assurance is not a matter of persuading ourselves; it is the direct ministry of the Spirit (Galatians 4:6; 1 John 4:13).

His gifts and fruit
The New Testament speaks of the 'gifts' of the Spirit and the 'fruit' of the Spirit.

❝ *It is usually said that there are nine gifts of the Spirit. (I suppose because Paul lists nine in 1 Corinthians 12). Actually Paul mentions no less than 17 (1 Corinthians 12:4-11, 27-31; Romans 12:3-8; Ephesians 4:7-11). And these are not natural talents*

merely, but gifts imparted by the Holy Spirit to fit the believer for his place in the body of Christ. They are like pipes on a great organ, permitting the musician wide scope and range to produce music of the finest quality. But they are, I repeat, more than talents. They are spiritual gifts. **❞**
A.W. Tozer

Some Christians today believe that the gifts were withdrawn by God at the end of the apostolic age: others believe they are still given today. It is possible to emphasize one or two of the seventeen gifts out of all proportion and become guilty of what Dr Tozer calls

❝ *shameless exhibitionism, a tendency to depend upon experiences instead of upon Christ, and often a lack of ability to distinguish the works of the flesh from the operations of the Spirit.* **❞**

The dove is another symbol of the Holy Spirit (Matt.3:16).

The fruit of the Spirit is love, joy, peace, patience, kindness, goodness, faithfulness, gentleness and self-control. **99**
Galatians 5:22.

Not all Christians will possess the *gifts* of the Spirit; God gives them to whom He wills (1 Corinthians 12:11, 30-31; 14:1). But the *fruit* of the Spirit God wishes to see in *all* His children. It signifies those spiritual qualities which are the result of a life submitted in loving obedience to the directions of the Holy Spirit as found in Scripture. As we live close to the Lord Jesus, and draw our life and strength from Him, so this fruit will be cultivated and will grow (John 15:1-17).

13
The Trinity

The Christian believes in God the Father, God the Son, and God the Holy Spirit.

⁶⁶ This is the God whom Christians worship — the Triune Jehovah. The heart of Christian faith in God is the revealed mystery of the Trinity. Trinitas is a Latin word meaning 'three-ness'. Christianity rests on the doctrine of the trinitas, the three-ness, the tri-personality, of God.⁹⁹
J.I. Packer

We do not believe in three Gods; there is only one God (1 Timothy 2:5). How do we explain this? The simple answer is that we shall never explain it in terms that will satisfy our understanding, for here is a profound mystery. Although the actual word *Trinity* is not found in the Scriptures, the doctrine is found there. But it is a revealed doctrine, one to which the Scriptures allude and point rather than defining it for us. The nature of the doctrine makes this inevitable, for it is not possible to define the Godhead. Professor Kenneth Grider was perfectly correct when he wrote:

⁶⁶ Off with our shoes, please, for the Holy Trinity is holy ground. Away with figured syllogisms [that is, trying to reason it out] and ordinary arithmetic: here, logic and mathematics do not suffice. The need is rather for a listening ear, an obedient heart (John 7:17), rapt adoration, a careful engagement with the Holy Scriptures.⁹⁹

Augustine in the fifth century gave a great deal of time to thinking about the doctrine of the Trinity. One day, as he was walking along the sea-shore, he saw a boy digging in the sand. He asked him what he was trying to do, and the youngster replied that he wanted to empty the sea into his hole in the sand. This set Augustine thinking: 'Am I not trying to do the same thing as this child, in seeking to exhaust with my reason the infinity of God and to collect it within the limits of my own mind?'

In approaching this truth, therefore, we have to accept the great limitations to which we are subject. To counterbalance this, some have tried to think of analogies or pictures to illustrate

the Trinity as having one substance in three forms (e.g. water, ice and steam, or the three leaves of a shamrock). But God in His trinitarian form is unique; there is nothing in human experience like Him, and therefore there can be no real analogy.

" *We are deeply conscious that the Trinity is a mystery beyond our comprehension. The glory of God is incomprehensible. There are no analogies for what we have been describing. There is no way we can picture this truth. You can have three men, each of whom is equally human, and distinct from the other. But at the end of the day you still have three men, and not one. The three Persons of the Godhead are each equally God, and distinct from each other. The mystery is that you still have but one God.* "
Stuart Olyott

We believe that there is only one God, but that in the Godhead there are three Persons — Father, Son and Holy Spirit. Each Person is distinct; each is equally God. He is the Triune God, the Three-in-One. And we believe this because this is how God has revealed Himself to us in the Bible.

The truth that there is more than one Person in the Godhead is revealed to us in the Bible by the use of the word 'us' in Genesis (1:26; 3:22; 11:7). We have already seen the passage in Isaiah 6 variously described as referring to the Father (Isaiah 6), the Son (John 12) and the Spirit (Acts 28). At the baptism of Jesus we see the Trinity in action: the Son is being baptized, the Father speaks, and the Spirit descends. At the end of Matthew's Gospel (28:19) we have the famous baptismal formula, and Paul concludes 2 Corinthians with the lovely benediction, *'May the grace of the Lord Jesus Christ, and the love of God, and the fellowship of the Holy Spirit be with you all.'*

" *As we have seen, Paul clearly believed in the unity of God. He invokes all three Persons in his benediction, and clearly accepts God's three-ness. He can do this, while still maintaining God's one-ness. We say it again, although the word 'Trinity' is not found in the Bible, the doctrine of the Trinity is there for all to see.* "
Stuart Olyott

14
Sin

Sin's origin

Man was made in the image of God. This does not mean a physical resemblance. It refers rather to the capacity given to man at creation to know and enjoy God. Man was created in righteousness, and it was his privilege to enjoy fellowship and communion with God.

This fellowship was shattered by what is commonly called *the fall of man*. The events are related in the third chapter of Genesis. The story of Adam and Eve is generally regarded as a myth today. That is a tragic mistake, for the events recorded in that chapter have a greater bearing on your life today than anything that is currently happening. It is here that we have the origin of sin in man's nature.

God is holy. There is no sin in Him. He cannot sin. God cannot lie, cheat, envy, or sin in any way. But more than that: not only is He not evil; He is righteous and just. God is light, and in Him there is no darkness at all. He dwells in the realm of light. His holiness is a consuming fire. It follows, then, that everything God does or produces will be good. The world

that God created and everything in it, including man, was good. Sin was no part of creation; it is an intrusion into God's world, and is inspired by the devil.

The holy God gave man righteous and just laws by which to live a full and happy life. But sin is a rejection of God's character and authority; it is an attack on the holiness of God. *'Everyone who sins breaks the law; in fact, sin is lawlessness'* (1 John 3:4).

This is clearly illustrated in Genesis 3. We read in Genesis 2:17 of the restriction which God put upon man in the paradise of Eden: *'You must not eat from the tree of the knowledge of good and evil, for when you eat of it you will surely die.'* That is the clear command and warning given by God. The devil comes to Eve in the form of a serpent, and his first approach is to cast doubt on the command: *'Did God really say?'* (3:1). Then he contradicts the warning: *'You will not surely die'* (3:4). Finally, he openly attacks the goodness of God (3:5) by suggesting that God has imposed this restriction because He is afraid that Adam and Eve will become like Him, and then He will have rivals.

Adam and Eve are deceived. They disobey God, and sin becomes part of man's nature: *'Sin entered the world through one man, and death through sin, and in this way death came to all men, because all sinned'* (Romans 5:12). In other words, it became part of our human nature — that nature that we have all inherited from Adam — to rebel against God. But more than that: the serious consequences of such rebellion — what the apostle Paul calls 'death through sin' — also became part of our experience.

Sin's consequences

The consequences of the entering in of sin into man's nature are enormous. Here are some of them.

1. Lost Privileges

When sin entered in, man lost many precious privileges.

☐ He lost **peace with God.** *'I was afraid . . . so I hid'* (Genesis 3:10). Men are still afraid of God and are still hiding from Him. Many try to camouflage this by denying that God exists.

☐ He lost **access to God.** Sin bars us from the holy presence of God. Genesis 3 ends with man being driven from Eden. This is what the Scriptures mean when they say that

man is spiritually dead: he is without God in the world. And nothing has changed; the holy God will no more tolerate sin in us than He did in Adam. Of heaven He says: *'Nothing impure will ever enter it, nor will anyone who does what is shameful or deceitful'* (Revelation 21:27).

☐ He lost **eternal life.** We have already seen that God warned Adam that if he sinned he would die (Genesis 2:17). Adam did sin, and immediately he knew spiritual death; he died to God. This was later followed by physical death.

2. A polluted nature

Another of the terrible effects of the entrance of sin is that it pollutes every part of man's nature.

☐ Sin affects our **mind.** *'The sinful mind is hostile to God. It does not submit to God's law, nor can it do so'* (Romans 8:7). *'Man without the Spirit does not accept the things that come from the Spirit of God, for they are foolishness to him, and he cannot understand them'* (1 Corinthians 2:14).

☐ Sin also affects our **freedom.** *'Everyone who sins is a slave to sin'* (John 8:34).

☐ And sin affects our **desires.** *'All of us also lived among them at one time, gratifying the cravings of our sinful nature and following its desires and thoughts'* (Ephesians 2:3).

This is not a pretty picture, but it is an accurate description of the effects of sin upon human nature.

3. The wrath of God

But the entry of sin has even worse consequences than those we have mentioned. Not only does sin make man a stranger to God, an enemy of God, *'dead in . . . transgressions and sins'* (Ephesians 2:1), but *sin puts him under the wrath of God.*

☐ God is angry with sin. *'The wrath of God is being revealed from heaven against all the godlessness and wickedness of men'* (Romans 1:18). Worse still, men are *'by nature objects of wrath'* (Ephesians 2:3).

15

The Atonement

> **"** *'Atonement' is one of the difficult words in the Scripture. It is found chiefly in the Old Testament and stands for the idea of 'covering'. Sin is thus said to be 'covered', or atoned for, by the Old Testament sacrifices described in Exodus and Leviticus. These sacrifices were designed symbolically to make amends for sin, and they pointed towards the effects of the work of Christ. The claims of God's holy law were satisfied by the Lord Jesus Christ, first in His life of obedience, and then in His suffering of the 'wages of sin' in His own body on the tree, and so He made an 'atonement' for man's sin.* **"**
>
> E.F. Kevan

The atonement is God's answer to man's sin and, as such, the *only* effective answer to human sinfulness and guilt.

The doctrine of the atonement is the biblical teaching on what the death of the Lord Jesus Christ means. The death of Jesus was clearly predetermined by God (Acts 2:23; 1 Peter 1:20), and He did so because of His love (John 3:16; Romans 5:8). If God did not love us, He would never have sent His Son to atone for our sin.

Old Testament pictures

In the Old Testament God shows us several pictures of what the death of Jesus means. There is the picture in Genesis 22 of the sacrifice of Isaac; but Isaac is spared when God Himself provides a lamb. The story of the Passover in Exodus 12 again illustrates that the shed blood of a lamb saves God's people from death. God promises them, *'When I see the blood, I will pass over you'* — that is, *'My judgment will not touch you'* (verse 13). The apostle Paul likens the death of Jesus to this by describing Christ as 'our Passover lamb' (1 Corinthians 5:7).

One of the most vivid pictures in

An ancient olive tree in Gethsemane.

the Old Testament is that of the Day of Atonement in Leviticus 16. Note especially verses 21 and 22: the high priest puts his hand on the head of the scapegoat and confesses the sin of the people, and symbolically that sin is transferred to the innocent victim, who takes it away. Isaac Watts captures this picture beautifully in one of his hymns:

But Christ, the heavenly Lamb,
  Takes all our sins away;
A sacrifice of nobler name,
  And richer blood than they.

My faith would lay her hand
  On that dear head of Thine,
While like a penitent I stand,
  And there confess my sin.

These pictures bring before us two basic truths about the atonement:

when Jesus died, it was an act of *substitution* and *propitiation*.

Substitution
Ponder carefully the following statements:

☐ *'The Lord has laid on him the iniquity of us all'* (Isaiah 53:6).
☐ *'He himself bore our sins in his body on the tree'* (1 Peter 2:24).
☐ *'God made him who had no sin to be sin for us'* (2 Corinthians 5:21).

Each of them tells us that Jesus died in our place. We deserved to die, but He died instead of us, He became our Substitute. He became the 'scapegoat', the innocent victim bearing the guilt of others and suffering their just punishment. This was God's plan, and it made salvation possible for guilty sinners.

Propitiation

In the Authorized Version, the first part of Romans 3:25 reads, *'Whom God hath set forth to be a propitiation through faith in his blood'*. This word 'propitiation' is not found in most modern translations of the Bible; instead, the New International Version uses the phrase 'sacrifice of atonement'. The word 'propitiation' means that on the cross, bearing our sin and guilt, Jesus faced the wrath of God instead of us, and paid fully on our behalf the debt we owed to the broken law of God. On the cross our Saviour cried, *'My God, my God, why have you forsaken me?'* (Matthew 27:46). The holy God forsook His Son because He was our sin-bearer — *'God made him who had no sin to be sin for us'* (2 Corinthians 5:21). Jesus was *'stricken by God, smitten by him, and afflicted'* (Isaiah 53:4). On the cross the Old Testament prophecy of Zechariah 13:7 was being fulfilled: *'"Awake, O sword, against my shepherd . . ." declares the Lord Almighty. "Strike the shepherd . . ."'* The sword was the sword of judgment, and in Matthew 26:31 Jesus tells us clearly that this verse speaks of Him.

In other words, at Calvary our Lord made it possible for a holy God to be propitious — or favourably inclined — towards us, even though we were sinners and had broken His holy law. God dealt with the problem of sin in the only way that could satisfy His holy justice and enable Him to move in and break the power of Satan in sinners' lives.

An incense altar of the type used by the Canaanites at the time of Joshua's conquest of the Promised Land.

Blood

Another word that is crucial to a true understanding of the atonement is the word 'blood'. You will notice that the New Testament writers, when referring to His atoning death, are always speaking of the blood of Jesus (Acts 20:28; Romans 3:25; 5:9; Ephesians 1:7; 2:13; Colossians 1:20; Hebrews 9:14; 1 Peter 1:2,19; 1 John 1:7; Revelation 1:5; 5:9).

66 *Why does the Apostle Paul, and why do the other writers talk about His* blood *and not simply say His* death? *Why say particularly His* blood? *This is the vital question, because it is obviously something that is done quite deliberately. And there is an obvious answer to the question. The term* blood *is used rather than* death *in order to bring this teaching concerning our Lord, and the way in which He redeems us, into line with the whole of the teaching of the Old Testament with regard to sacrifices.* **99**
D.M. Lloyd-Jones

The point is that it was not merely the death of Jesus that atones for sin, but His *sacrificial* death. He did not die of natural causes; His death was not an accident; but He died as the sacrifice for our sin. Therefore, the sacrificial language and pictures of the Old Testament are fundamental to a correct understanding of the atoning death of Jesus in the New Testament.

66 *For centuries, the cross has been the undisputed symbol of Christianity. By the cross we do not mean a crucifix, which is a symbol of weakness and defeat, but an empty cross, which is a symbol of victory. The cross is the place where Jesus made atonement for our sin, and the purpose of His death was to bring us to God (1 Peter 3:18).* **99**

16
Grace

If we do not understand the New Testament meaning of the word 'grace', we shall never understand the New Testament. Grace is the substance and the very heart of its message. This is easily demonstrated:

☐ God is a God of grace: 1 Peter 5:10.
☐ Jesus brings grace to the world: John 1:17.
☐ The Holy Spirit is a Spirit of grace: Hebrews 10:29.
☐ Salvation is a product of grace: Titus 2:11.
☐ Justification is by grace: Romans 3:24.
☐ Redemption is according to grace: Ephesians 1:7.

What, then, *is* grace? It is the free, unmerited, undeserved favour of God to sinners. It is God showing goodness to a people who deserve only judgment and condemnation. The sinner does not come looking for grace from God, but God, in grace, comes looking for the sinner.

Grace exists, and is necessary, for two reasons: the character of man, and the character of God.

Though man was created in the image of God, able to know and enjoy Him, when man sinned he became separated from God, and sin has since dominated all his actions. He is now an alien to God his Maker, and because of his sinful character he can do nothing about it. God's character, on the other hand, is such that He cannot condone or overlook sin. His holiness, truth and justice demand that man must be dealt with as he is, and that sin must be punished.

These two factors, taken on their own, would condemn all men to an eternity in hell. But God's character is also such that though He hates sin, yet He loves the guilty sinner who deserves His judgment. Divine love therefore plans salvation, and divine grace provides salvation. Grace is necessary, because without it sinful man has no hope; and grace is possible because of the loving and merciful character of God.

Once this truth is grasped and understood, grace becomes the most thrilling thing there is.

❝ *To the New Testament writers, grace is a wonder. Their sense of*

man's corruption and demerit before God, and of the reality and justice of His wrath against sin, is so strong that they find it simply staggering that there should be such a thing as grace at all — let alone grace that was so costly to God as the grace of Calvary. **"**
J.I. Packer

The hymn-writers share the same wonder, describing it as 'amazing grace' (John Newton and Charles Wesley), 'abounding grace' (Augustus Toplady), 'a charming sound' (Doddridge), 'sovereign grace' (John Kent, Isaac Watts and Charles Wesley).

Grace and salvation

Grace and salvation belong together as cause and effect (Ephesians 2:5; Titus 2:11). Grace is the cause of salvation. The gospel centres upon the great doctrine of justification by faith: it is in justification that we receive pardon for sin and peace with God, and justification is the product of divine grace (Romans 3:24). Grace flows from the tender heart of God the Father, and it is embodied in Jesus Christ the Son of God. It is Jesus who makes grace a reality by fulfilling the dictates of grace: He dies, the just for the unjust; He appeases the holy wrath of God; He sheds His blood to cover our sin, and He takes our sin away. All this is because of grace.

Olney Vicarage in Buckinghamshire. John Newton was a curate here from 1764 until 1779, when he began a new ministry in London.

The grace of God is proclaimed in the gospel. The gospel announces with uncompromising clarity that unless we are saved by grace, we cannot be saved at all. It addresses men as guilty, lost, condemned sinners, and it takes no account of man's achievements. All those things about which he loves to boast — morality, religious fervour, devout sincerity — the gospel tosses aside as filthy rags,

declaring that what a man needs to be right with God is grace, and grace alone.

66 *Salvation is not in any sense God's response to anything in us. It is not something that we in any sense deserve or merit. The whole essence of the teaching at this point, and everywhere in all the New Testament, is that we have no sort or kind of right whatsoever to salvation, that the whole glory of salvation is, that though we deserved nothing but punishment and hell and banishment out of the sight of God to all eternity, yet God, of His own love and grace and wondrous mercy, has granted us this salvation. Now this is the entire meaning of this term 'grace'.* 99

D.M. Lloyd-Jones

Irresistible grace

The term 'irresistible grace' does not mean that man cannot reject the gospel; he can and he does. Very few people are converted the first time they hear the gospel; but grace will not take no for an answer and begins to work on the sinner's mind and conscience. Irresistible grace does not mean that God saves a man against his will; rather, grace seeks to change the will, until the sinner wants salvation more than anything else.

66 Not only is grace irresistible, it must be irresistible. For if grace were not irresistible no one would ever have been saved. That follows of necessity from the fact that we were dead spiritually, and were at enmity to God, hating His truth.

How can we be saved therefore? There is only one answer — the power of grace is irresistible. **99**
D.M. Lloyd-Jones

Grace is not a way of helping sinners to be saved; it is God's way of salvation. In other words, grace is not given to aid or assist us; it is the power of God to save us.

66 Grace is a provision for men who are so fallen that they cannot lift the axe of justice, so corrupt that they cannot change their own natures, so averse to God that they cannot turn to Him, so blind that they cannot see Him, and so dead that He Himself must open their graves and lift them into resurrection. **99**
G.S. Bishop

17
Regeneration

When Jesus told Nicodemus, *'You must be born again'* (John 3:7), He was speaking of the need for regeneration.

❝ *Regeneration is the beginning of all saving grace in us, and all saving grace in exercise on our part proceeds from the fountain of regeneration. We are not born again by faith or repentance or conversion: we repent and believe because we have been regenerated.* **❞**
John Murray

The effect of sin upon human nature is so thorough that the Bible describes man as 'dead' in sin. That is, man is dead to God, he is spiritually dead, he does not know God, and as long as he remains in that condition he cannot know God. There is nothing he can do to please God (Romans 8:8), and he cannot even come to God (John 6:44,65). When it uses the term 'dead in

Soviet Christians at an early morning baptismal service near Odessa.

sin', the Bible means what it says: man is helpless, hopeless and useless; because he is dead in sin, he cannot believe, or exercise faith, or repent. It is therefore of the utmost importance that man's condition be changed: he must be regenerated; life must be given to his dead soul. If there is to be spiritual life, there must be a spiritual birth. This is the only way any real change can be brought about, for

❝ *regeneration is the basis of all change in the heart and life. It is a stupendous change because it is God's recreative act.* **❞**
John Murray

Regeneration, or new birth, is God giving to man who is dead in sin new life. This is a 'must', without which nothing else is spiritually possible. It is not simply a man changing his mind about God; it is something God does to man and in man (Ezekiel 36:26-27). And it is so thorough that the man becomes a new person (2 Corinthians 5:17).

Jesus tells us that the new birth is the work of the Holy Spirit (John 3:1-12). Read carefully verse 8 of John chapter 3.

❝ *Nobody on earth can direct the wind. It acts with complete independence. It cannot even be seen. That it must be there you know, for, in striking any object it makes a sound. Its source and its ultimate goal or destination no one knows. Jesus adds, So is everyone who is born of the Spirit. Its operation is sovereign,*

incomprehensible, and mysterious. **❞**
William Hendriksen

Signs of Life

Dr James Packer says, *'The signs whereby a regenerate person may be known correspond to the natural actions of the newborn child.'*

The first thing a new-born baby does is cry. It cries out for its needs to be satisfied by the one who has given it life. The new-born Christian likewise cries out to God; he prays, knowing his complete dependence upon his Lord.

Secondly, just as the baby feeds, so the new Christian has a hunger for the milk of God's Word (1 Peter 2:2).

The baby also sleeps. There is a beautiful peace about a baby sleeping, and the born-again Christian knows and delights in the peace he has with God through Jesus Christ.

Lastly, the baby grows. For the Christian, spiritual growth is a sign of spiritual life (2 Thessalonians 1:3).

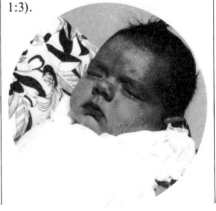

18
Repentance and faith

We are dealing with repentance and faith together, because they cannot really be separated. Where there is true faith, there will inevitably be repentance. Sometimes it is asked which comes first; but, as they are inter-dependent, this is a pointless question — faith and repentance cannot exist without one another.

Repentance

Repentance is not a case of trying your best to get rid of all the sin in your life and put things right. What repentance means is this: the sinner, conscious of his guilt and aware of God's mercy in Christ, turns from his sin to God. The repentant sinner finds himself loathing and hating sin and longing to live in obedience to God. When a man repents, he will cry to God for mercy and pardon.

Without repentance there is no salvation. The first words of Jesus when He began preaching were *'Repent, for the kingdom of heaven is near'* (Matthew 4:17), and this note is clearly sounded in the apostles' ministry — *'God . . . now commands all people everywhere to repent'* (Acts 17:30).

Repentance has two sides: it is a turning *from* sin, and *to* God. For true repentance both these elements are essential. A man can turn from sin without turning to God. He may see the value of 'turning over a new leaf' and decide to refrain from certain bad habits. No doubt this will do him good in a variety of ways, but *spiritually* it will be useless. On the other hand, a man may turn to God and cry for mercy, but have no intention of leaving his sin. His eyes may be wet with tears, but his heart as hard as stone.

True repentance involves seeing sin for what it really is: not just a character defect, but a permanent posture of rebellion against the love and care and righteous authority of a holy God. It is this new understanding of God and of one's own sin that leads to true repentance. There will also be a great desire to break with the past and to live in future only to please God and for His glory. That is repentance.

Faith

John Murray writes about faith as follows:

155

❝ Regeneration is the act of God and of God alone. But faith is not the act of God; it is not God who believes in Christ for salvation, it is the sinner. It is by God's grace that a person is able to believe, but faith is an activity on the part of the person and of him alone. In faith we receive and rest upon Christ alone for salvation. ❞

Faith is a gift of God (Ephesians 2:8), and it comes by hearing the gospel (Romans 10:17). But we are not saved because of our faith; it is Jesus Christ who saves us, not faith. Faith is the channel through which salvation comes from God to us.

Faith is an unwavering trust in the Lord Jesus Christ as the only Saviour to deal with sin. It is not merely an intellectual assent to a set of doctrines, but a coming to Christ in repentance, crying for mercy. Faith hears the truth of the gospel, believes it and then acts upon it. Saving faith progresses from an intellectual acceptance of certain facts to a real trusting in Christ and what He has done on our behalf and for our salvation. Faith is a response of the mind and the heart to the Saviour of whom the gospel speaks.

We have so far considered repentance and faith only in terms of salvation. But they do not finish there, for the Christian experiences them both working daily in his life. For instance, he often knows a deeper conviction of sin and repentance *after* conversion than he knew before. Read Psalm 51 as

Preaching the gospel in the open air at Aberystwyth.

an example of this. Matthew Henry said:

66 *Repentance is a daily duty. He that repents every day for the sins of every day, when he comes to die will have the sins of only one day to repent of. Short reckonings make long friends.* **99**

Faith also is something that grows and develops. The Christian life is to be a life of faith, as daily we learn to trust the Lord and depend upon Him.

66 *True faith is not passive but active. It requires that we meet certain conditions, that we allow the teachings of Christ to dominate our total lives from the moment we believe. The man of saving faith must be willing to be different from others. The effort to enjoy the benefits of redemption while enmeshed in the world is futile. We must choose one or the other; and faith quickly makes its choice, one from which there is no retreat.* **99**
A.W. Tozer

19
Reconciliation

What is the meaning of the term 'reconciliation'?

‟ To reconcile means to bring together again persons who had previously fallen out; to replace alienation, hostility and opposition by a new relationship of favour, goodwill and peace; and so to transform the attitude of the persons reconciled towards each other and to set their subsequent mutual dealings on a wholly new footing. ‟
J.I. Packer

On four occasions the New Testament speaks of the work and ministry of Christ in terms of reconciliation (Romans 5:10; 2 Corinthians 5:18-21; Ephesians 2:16; Colossians 1:22)

Reconciliation is necessary because of the hostility that exists between God and man through sin. Notice the language Paul uses when he speaks of reconciliation: 'enemies' (Romans 5:10), 'hostility' (Ephesians 2:16), 'alienated' and 'enemies' (Colossians 1:21). It is often claimed that all men are the children of God, and that God is

the Father of all; but the Word of God teaches that the opposite is the case. Man is by nature an enemy of God, and because of human sin, God refuses to have man in His presence. He does not call us men His children, but sinners, rebels and enemies. Sin has brought about a situation in which man disagrees with God, and God disagrees with man.

There is therefore a need for reconciliation. Sin, which is the cause of the problem, has to be dealt with and removed.

Since it is quite beyond the capability of man to deal with sin, reconciliation has to be the work

General Douglas MacArthur signs the instrument of surrender on board the USS Missouri at the end of the Second World War.

of God. God must deal with human sin in such a way as to be able to bring us to Himself in peace, as His redeemed children. And all this God accomplishes in and through Jesus Christ. Reconciliation is:

☐ through the death of Jesus (Romans 5:10),
☐ through the cross of Jesus (Ephesians 2:16),
☐ through the blood of Jesus (Colossians 1:20).

Now read again 2 Corinthians 5:18-21, and note the following:

1. God does not count men's sins against them (verse 19). Sin deserves punishment, and God's law demands that each man be held personally responsible for his sin. As each sin is added to his account to await God's judgment, the debt grows like individual items on a bill. But in His work of reconciliation God removes every single item from the bill, so that we have nothing to pay! Our sins are not accounted against us.
2. What then happens to our sin? Does God just forget it? No, God is just, and He cannot do that. The sins have to be answered for, the debt has to be paid. God's answer to this is to count our sin against Jesus: 'God made him who had no sin to be sin for us' (verse 21) — or, as Isaiah says, *'The*

Meter Readings Darlleniadau r mesurydd		Units Consumed	Unit Charges Prisiau unedau		VAT	£
Previous Blaenorol	Present Presennol	Unedau a losgwyd	@7.67 1000	@5.49 99	0 0	82.13 11.25
66023	67122	1099				
QUARTERLY STANDING CHARGE						

		MOVING HOUSE?	Value excluding VAT	VAT
			£93.38	0

Amount DUE £93.38

YOUR LOCAL DISTRICT OFFICE I
W.CENTRAL DISTRICT
29 YSTRAD ROAD
FFORESTFACH   TEL.SWANSEA 5
SWANSEA   SA5 4LH

S.W.A.E.B. 13 APR 1987 PAID

Lord has laid on him the iniquity of us all' (53:6).

3. Reconciliation is not yet complete. Our sin and guilt, which have been credited to Jesus, are now dealt with by God. He pours out upon our Substitute, the Lord Jesus Christ, the punishment our sin deserves. He is treated as the sinner should be treated, and Jesus dies instead of us (Isaiah 53:5). This is why reconciliation is said to be through the death, the cross and the blood of Jesus.

4. Now that our sin has been dealt with, the righteousness of Jesus is credited to us (verse 21). We are treated as children of God and joint heirs with Christ (Romans 8:17). We are reconciled.

My God is reconciled,
   His pardoning voice I hear;
He owns me for His child,
   I can no longer fear;
With confidence I now draw nigh,
And Father, Abba, Father! cry.
Charles Wesley

" Reconciliation means the ending of enmity and the making of peace and friendship between persons previously opposed. God and men were at enmity with each other by reason of men's sins; but God has acted in Christ to reconcile sinners to Himself through the cross. The achieving of reconciliation was a task which Christ completed at Calvary. In virtue of Christ's finished work of atonement, God now invites sinners everywhere to receive the reconciliation and thus be reconciled to Himself. Believers enjoy through Christ an actual reconcilement with God which is perfect and final."
J.I. Packer

20
Redemption

To *redeem* means to set someone free from captivity or slavery by the payment of a ransom price.

All mankind is in captivity to sin. We are slaves to our own corrupt and depraved nature. It is a bondage of the mind, the will and the spirit so powerful that, left to ourselves, freedom would be impossible (Psalm 49:7-8). The Lord Jesus Christ came into the world to purchase this freedom for us. He gave His life as a ransom for many (Matthew 20:28), and the price He paid was His own blood (Ephesians 1:7; 1 Peter 1:18-19).

Redemption means more than purchase. A man may purchase a slave, but that slave would still remain a slave; though his master may change, his condition of slavery would be the same. But redemption gives freedom. When Christ redeems a person, not only does his master change, but he now obeys his new Lord and Master (Romans 6:22) with a free will. He has been set free from his old, empty way of life (1 Peter 1:18), and he now seeks to serve his new Master, Jesus Christ, with a glad and free heart.

Redemption in the Old Testament

The idea of redemption is firmly rooted in the Old Testament. Read the following verses: Exodus 6:6-7; 15:12-13; Psalm 77:14-15; Jeremiah 50:33-34.

❝ *In passages like these there is an emphasis on the power of God, a power that He puts forward on behalf of His people. Being as great as He is, He could rescue them with effortless ease. But because He loves His people He puts forth His power. He saves them at cost. It is this that gives the use of the redemption terminology its point.* **❞**
Leon Morris

Redemption is a costly business. In the preceding passages we see God as the Redeemer exerting all His mighty power to bring about redemption. In other Old Testament passages redemption is used in the sphere of human relationships, and each time there is a price to pay (Leviticus 25:25-31; Ruth 4:2-4).

A Nosu tribesman and his young Chinese slave. ▶

162

❝ *Our study of the use of the redemption terminology in the Old Testament then leads us to the conclusion that it is concerned with release on payment of a price. It is not used of simple release. For that other terms were available and were in use. The idea of payment of a price (the 'ransom') is basic to all the redemption words.* **❞**
Leon Morris

Christ the Redeemer
Without the redemption of Christ man is in a hopeless plight:

❝ *The whole world is in a state of slavery to sin and to Satan; it is under the dominion of Satan. That is the term used. We are in bondage to the law which condemns us, having told us that, if we could keep it and honour it, it would save us. Its demands, its penalties, are plain and clear, but there is no man or collection of men that can ever pay the price of its demands. That is the fundamental teaching of the whole Bible, we are all by nature 'under the law' and in a state of condemnation.* **❞**
D.M. Lloyd-Jones

Jesus had paid the ransom price that can set sinners free from the bondage of the law (Galatians 3:13). The price has been paid once and for all (Hebrews 9:14). This act of redemption by Jesus on the cross is the only means of salvation for anyone, and that includes those of the Old Testament era (Hebrews 9:15).

Christ redeems us from:
- [ ] all wickedness (Titus 2:14)
- [ ] the grip of sin (Romans 6:18,22)
- [ ] the old life (1 Peter 1:18)
- [ ] the curse of the law (Galatians 3:13)
- [ ] the bondage of the law (Galatians 4:5)
- [ ] death (Job 5:20)
- [ ] hell (Psalm 49:15)

21
Justification

Justification is the sovereign work of God whereby He declares the guilty sinner to be righteous and the rightful demands of the law satisfied.

Let us examine this definition:

☐ **sovereign work of God** — God does it all; the sinner plays no part at all (Romans 3:24; 4:4,5).

☐ **declares** — the judge pronounces a legal verdict.

☐ **guilty sinner** — guilty by nature (Ephesians 2:1-3) and guilty by action (Romans 3:10-23).

☐ **righteous** — right with God (Romans 5:1).

☐ **demands of the law** — God's law demands eternal death for the sinner (Romans 6:23).

☐ **satisfied** — legally and justly satisfied by the atoning death of Jesus (Romans 5:18-21; 3:26).

❝ What does justification by faith mean? This is the doctrine which tells us that God has contrived a way whereby men and women can be saved and reconciled unto Himself. It is all of His doing. It tells us that God, on the basis of what He has done in His Son, our blessed Lord and Saviour, freely forgives, and absolves from all their sin, all who believe the gospel. But it does not stop at that; they are furthermore 'clothed with the righteousness of Jesus Christ' and declared to be just and righteous in God's sight. It is not only negative, there is this positive aspect also. We are clothed with the righteousness of Christ which is 'imputed' to us, 'put to our account', and so we stand accepted in the sight of God. As Romans 5 verse 19 puts it, we are 'constituted' righteous people in the presence of this holy and righteous God. ❞
D.M. Lloyd-Jones

Justification has to do with our standing before the holy God. It does not make the sinner any different. It is crucial that you understand this. Listen again to Dr Lloyd-Jones:

❝ It does not mean that we are made righteous, but rather that God regards us as righteous and declares us to be righteous. This has often been a difficulty to many people. They say that because they are conscious of sin within they

Dr D. Martyn Lloyd-Jones.

cannot be in a justified state; but anyone who speaks like that shows immediately that he has no understanding of this great and crucial doctrine of justification. Justification makes no actual change in us; it is a declaration by God concerning us. It is not something that results from what we do but rather something that is done for us. We have only been made righteous in the sense that God regards us as righteous, and pronounces us to be righteous. **99**

A group of Soviet Christians at an open air service. Although they have suffered persecution from the authorities, they still rejoice in the God who freed them from the guilt of sin.

Someone may ask: if justification does not make me any better, what is the point of it? The point is this: as soon as you are justified you are right with God! You could go to heaven there and then. You are accepted in Christ (Ephesians 1:6 *Authorized Version*).

But God does not stop there. He immediately begins in you the process of change, called sanctification, that will make you a different person. Justification frees you from the *guilt* of sin and its condemnation. It is a once-for-all declaration by God. Then, the moment you are justified, the process of sanctification begins which will free you from the *power* of sin.

22
Sanctification

The word *sanctification* is used in several different ways in the Bible, but in the New Testament it is used primarily to describe that process by which the Christian is purified in heart and mind.

☐ God's will for you is sanctification (1 Thessalonians 4:3).
☐ This means holiness (1 Thessalonians 4:7).
☐ This is a work which God accomplishes in and through you (1 Thessalonians 5:23).

❝ *Sanctification [is] that gracious and continuous operation of the Holy Spirit, by which He delivers the justified sinner from the pollution of sin, renews his whole nature in the image of God, and enables him to perform good works.* **❞**
L. Berkhof

There is no such thing as instant sanctification. There is no easy formula to achieve holiness. Phrases like 'Let go and let God' may sound fine, but they are not quite what the Bible teaches.
God is the author of sanctification, not man.

Nevertheless, God requires *us* to co-operate with Him. It is *our* responsibility to strive for an ever-increasing sanctification by using the means which God has provided for us. Read 2 Corinthians 7:1; Colossians 3:5-14; 1 Peter 1:22.
No one attains to complete sanctification in this life (1 Kings 8:46; 1 John 1:8). Yet the Scripture tells us that the saints in heaven are completely free from the power of sin (Hebrews 12:23; Revelation 14:5). This means that our sanctification is completed either at death or immediately after.
As far as the present is concerned, sanctification means that the power of sin is being overcome in us. The dominion or reigning power of sin has already been broken. Read Romans 6. This great chapter reminds us that whereas we were once the slaves of sin (it dominated us, controlled us and dictated the pattern of our life), that has now changed. We are in Christ. We are dead to sin (verse 11). That is, the person that I was before, I no longer am. Before, I was under sin. Now that I am a new creature in Christ

Jesus, sin has no authority over me. It has no power to make me obey it.

This does not mean that sin does not bother the Christian. Of course it does, but because its absolute authority and reign have ceased, we can now triumph over it. We are no longer slaves of sin, under its heel and dominion. We are enemies of sin, fighting and resisting its evil influences. We do not obey it (verse 12). We do not yield to it (verse 13). We mortify (put to death) sin's advances in us (Romans 8:13; Colossians 3:5).

All this is not easy. It involves effort and determination, and it is only possible because *'we know*

More than 200,000 people in the city of Nairobi in Kenya live in slum housing, sometimes made only from plastic sheeting, cardboard, tins and mud. Christians need to show by their works that they care for people like these.

that our old self was crucified with him [Christ], so that the body of sin might be rendered powerless, that we should no longer be slaves to sin' (Romans 6:6).

Even though we are Christians, there remains much of the old, sinful nature in us. We must not pander to it. It must be resisted and fought, and our new nature must be allowed to rule (Ephesians 4:20-32). It is as we do this that our lives are made better, holier, and more Christlike, because sanctification affects every part of us:

☐ understanding : Jeremiah 31:33,34.
☐ will : Ezekiel 36:25-27.
☐ passions : Galatians 5:24.
☐ conscience : Hebrews 9:14.

God delights to see 'good works' in His people — not as a *means* of

salvation (Ephesians 2:8,9), but as the *product* of salvation that brings glory to God our Saviour (Matthew 5:16).

&& *'Good works' are the necessary evidence of faith. This is what James pressed for in his epistle in chapter 2. Look, for example, at verse 17:* 'Faith', *he says,* 'if it hath not works, is dead, being alone.' *In the next verse he says,* 'I will show thee my faith by my works.' *Again in verse 20 he says,* 'Faith without works is dead.' *'Good works', then, are the necessary evidence that a man is a true believer. The old commentator on the Bible, Matthew Henry, wrote,* 'If religion has done nothing for your tempers, it has done nothing for your souls.' *In Ephesians 2, verse 10, Paul says* 'For we are his workmanship, created in Christ Jesus unto good works, which God hath before ordained that we should walk in them.'**&&**
E.F. Kevan

Differences

The differences between justification and sanctification can be summed up as follows:
1. Justification is all of God. Man plays no part. But whilst sanctification is also the work of God, we are expected to co-operate.
2. Justification is instantaneous; it is a once-for-all thing. You are as justified now as you will ever be, and you are as justified as any other Christian. Sanctification, however, is a process. It begins at salvation and goes on for the rest of your life. The Christian can grow in sanctification, and he can also decline in it (backsliding). All Christians are at different stages of sanctification.

Salvation is like being pulled out of a raging sea when waves were about to engulf you. You have been saved and placed safely upon the rocks. The waves cannot harm you there. You are safe — safe on the Rock Christ Jesus.

But salvation is more than a rescue operation. You must now go on to enjoy the life you were saved for. You are on the rock, and in front of you is a seemingly unclimbable steep cliff. You realize you could no more climb that yourself than you could have got out of the water yourself. Again, I stress, you are safe on the rock, but you want to go on and upward to the fuller life. The question is, how? Then you see a rope hanging down from the top of the cliff, and you hear a voice shouting instructions to you and saying, 'You climb, and I will pull.'

That is sanctification. You are to climb over all the seemingly impossible obstacles that would try to keep you down, and at the same time God is drawing you upward and onward.

23
Election

Among Christians, the subject of election and predestination is undoubtedly one of the most controversial. Some believers love and cherish it as the most thrilling and humbling of doctrines; other believers will not tolerate it at any price and regard it as totally abhorrent.

Let us first define the subject:

❝ *Predestination is God's eternal purpose whereby He has foreordained whatever comes to pass (Ephesians 1:11). Election may be defined as God's eternal purpose to cause certain specific individuals to be in Christ the recipients of special grace, in order that they may live to God's glory and may obtain everlasting salvation (Luke 10:20; Acts 13:48; Romans 11:5; Ephesians 1:4; 2 Thessalonians 2:13).* **❞**
William Hendriksen

These things can only be true if God is a *sovereign* God: that is, a God who rules, not merely taking an interest in His creation, but actually governing it. The Bible teaches that this God, who neither slumbers nor sleeps, is at any given moment in full control of the affairs of the world. He reigns over it, not with His hands tied, waiting for the co-operation and permission of men, but as the Almighty God. Consider Isaiah 40 as one example of how the sovereignty of God is presented to us in the Scriptures. Here the prophet extols the sovereignty of God in relation to

☐ the physical world:verses 12 & 26,
☐ knowledge:verses 13 & 14,
☐ the nations of the world:verses 15-17,
☐ idols:verses 18-20,
☐ His people: verses 28-31.

He sums it all up in verses 21-25. *'Here is your God!',* says Isaiah; He is *'the Sovereign Lord'* (verses 9,10). It is not surprising, therefore, that such a God can predestinate and elect. All through the Bible we find Him doing so. For example:

☐ God chose Abraham: Nehemiah 9:7.
☐ God chose Israel: Deuteronomy 7:7; Isaiah 41:8-9; Amos 3:2.

☐ God chose the priests: Deuteronomy 18:5.
☐ God chose David: 1 Kings 8:16.
☐ God chose the apostles: John 6:70.
☐ God chooses His people: John 15:16.

Election and salvation

Jesus did not come into the world to make salvation possible; He came to save. There is an enormous difference between making something possible and actually doing it. Election in salvation simply means that God saves specific individuals.

❝ *God saves sinners. God — the Triune Jehovah, Father, Son and Spirit, three Persons working together in sovereign wisdom, power and love to achieve the salvation of a chosen people, the Father electing, the Son fulfilling the Father's will by redeeming, the Spirit executing the purpose of Father and Son by renewing. Saves — does everything, first to last, that is involved in bringing man from death in sin to life in glory: plans, achieves and communicates redemption, calls and keeps, justifies, sanctifies, glorifies. Sinners — men as God finds them, guilty, vile, helpless, powerless, unable to lift a finger to do God's will or better their spiritual lot. God saves sinners.* **❞**
J.I. Packer

Paul states this truth very clearly in Ephesians 1:4 — *'For he chose us in him before the creation of the world'* — and repeats it in verse 11 of that chapter. In the light of such clear teaching, why do some Christians find so much difficulty in accepting this doctrine? First, they say that election is unfair: why should God choose some and not others? Secondly, they argue that election removes human responsibility; so if a man is not saved, God cannot blame him.

It is interesting to note that in Romans 9, a passage which clearly teaches the doctrine of election, Paul both faces and answers these objections. Read carefully Romans 9:1-13. Paul follows this by asking, in verse 14, *'What then shall we say?'* - or in other words, 'What is our reaction to this?' He then poses and answers two questions:

1. 'Is God unjust?' (verse 14) - it is not fair, say some. His answer to this is twofold:
☐ This is what Scripture teaches, as illustrated by Exodus 33:19.
☐ Far from being unfair, election is an act of divine mercy.
God does not punish anyone unjustly. He did not make Pharaoh a sinner, any more than He made us sinners. We are all sinners by nature, and therefore we all deserve God's wrath. But God in His mercy saves some, and in His justice condemns others. So he who is saved cannot say, 'I am better than others', and he who is condemned must acknowledge that he is receiving only what his sin deserves.

2. 'Then why does God still blame us?' (verse 19) — that is, man cannot be held responsible, for

A statue of Rameses II, who may
have been the pharaoh at the time
of the Exodus.

who can resist His will? Paul's answer to this is that such an objection springs from ignorance of the true relationship between God and man (verse 20). God is our Creator, and who are we to dare to demand that God should answer to our reasoning? Who are we to dismiss something so clearly declared by God, simply because it is not acceptable to our little minds?

Foreknowledge

Some Christians, appealing to 1 Peter 1:2, argue that all that is meant by election is that God, because of His omniscience, foreknew who would believe. So it is not a case of God choosing people for salvation, but rather of Him seeing in advance what people would do and merely acknowledging it.

It is significant that Paul did not use this argument in Romans 9 when he was dealing with the objections people raise. It would have been a simple answer if it were true. But Paul did not use it because he knew that in the Bible the term 'foreknowledge' means that it was foreordained. In Acts 2:23, for example, we are told that the death of Christ was by *'God's set purpose and foreknowledge':* that means not that God foresaw what would happen to Jesus, but that He planned it. The same is true of Romans 8:29, where the whole argument is concerned with the sovereignty of God who calls sinners to salvation *'according to his purpose'* (verse 28). A further example is found in Romans 11:2. Paul is saying here that God will not reject His people — not because He knows something about them, but because He has chosen them. (That is what the whole chapter is about.) Finally, when we look at 1 Peter 1:2, we have to come to the same conclusion. The Greek word translated 'foreknowledge' in verse 2 is basically the same as that translated as 'chosen' in verse 20 (in the AV, 'foreordained') — and in the latter case, of course, it can only mean that God *planned* Christ's coming.

Election is one of the most thrilling and humbling truths in the Bible. Not only so, but it provides us with the greatest possible incentive for evangelism:

❝ *Were there no election, there would be no calling, and no conversions, and all evangelistic activity would fail. But as it is, we know, as we spread God's truth, that His Word will not return to Him void. He has sent it to be the means whereby He calls His elect, and it will prosper in the thing for which He has sent it.* **❞**
J.I. Packer

24
Eternal security

> **"** *It is vital and essential that we should be clear about this doctrine of glorification, for it is the ultimate end of our salvation. God forbid that any of us should stop short at forgiveness, or look at salvation negatively as merely being saved from hell. I do not want to minimize the value of that aspect of salvation; we can never thank God sufficiently for delivering us from death and hell and everlasting punishment. But that, according to the teaching of the Scripture, is only the first step, the mere beginning. The end is glorification.* **"**
>
> D.M. Lloyd-Jones

Eternal security means that we are not only saved, but we are also *safe*. The Christian can never lose the salvation that he has in the Lord Jesus Christ. He can backslide (and so lose the joy and sense of reality of his salvation), but he can never fall from grace (that is, lose his salvation).

If we rightly understand the New Testament doctrine of salvation, we shall see that eternal security is inevitable. Salvation is much more than forgiveness of sins — thank God, it *is* that, but it is more than that. When we are saved, we are also adopted into the family of God. Romans 8:15-17 and

Galatians 4:4-7 speak of this, and both passages tell us that salvation makes us heirs of God. What are we to inherit? Paul tells us in Romans 8:17 that we are to *'share in his glory'*.

The apostle Paul goes on to show us the four great links in the chain of salvation:

☐ **Predestination,** which leads to calling.
☐ **Calling,** which leads to justification.
☐ **Justification,** which leads to glorification.
☐ **Glorification** (Romans 8:30).

Each of these links is as strong and as certain as the others. And because of this, Paul is able to declare with absolute conviction that nothing can separate believers from the love of God (verses 38-39). He is delighting in the certainty of glorification, the certainty of going to heaven.

Jesus teaches the same truth in John 10:28-29, giving two reasons why the Christian cannot lose his salvation.

☐ **First,** the life which the Good Shepherd gives to His sheep is 'eternal life' (verse 28); and so, inevitably, 'they shall never perish'. How can they, if they have *eternal* life? The life which the common grace of God gives to all men is limited to seventy years or so (Psalm 90:10); but the life which the saving grace of God gives to His people is without limits — it is eternal. And, says Paul, the gifts of God are irrevocable (Romans 11:29). God will never change His mind and take His gift back, and our salvation is therefore eternally secure.

☐ **Secondly,** Jesus points us to the true basis of salvation by saying, in verse 29, *'My Father, who has given them to me'.* If you compare this with John 6:37,39 and John 17:2,6,9 you will see that here we have no isolated reference but a recurring phrase. And it is one that answers many questions. Where does the Good Shepherd get His sheep from? The Father gives them to Him. Why do the sheep follow the Shepherd? Because they hear His voice (John 10:27). Why is it that they hear His voice and others do not? Because there has been an operation of grace in their hearts, without which they cannot believe (verse 26).

Caernarfon Castle, Gwynedd.

The subject that runs right through the Bible is the glory of God and man's salvation. The glory of God in man's salvation is that, by His sovereign decree, God has chosen for Himself a people — a people who belong to Him by His choice, not theirs. The order in which this happens is stated by the Lord Jesus Christ in John 17:

☐ *'They were yours':* verse 6.
☐ *'You gave them to me':* verse 6.
☐ Jesus gives them eternal life: verse 2.

So, from beginning to end, salvation is the work of God - and the end of that salvation is that we should be presented *'before his glorious presence without fault and with great joy'* (Jude 24). The God who has done all this for us, said Jesus, is *'greater than all'* (John 10:29). The only way a Christian could be snatched from the hand of God would be for the Almighty God Himself to be defeated; and since He is greater than all, that is impossible. Our salvation, therefore, is eternally secure.

Difficulties

Some Christians have great difficulty in accepting this doctrine, and they argue against it by appealing to passages like Hebrews 6:4-8 and 10:26-29. These passages have caused genuine problems to many a Christian who would love to believe in eternal security. We know that the Scriptures do not contradict themselves, so what do these verses mean? By way of answer, consider first the words of Dr D.M. Lloyd-Jones:

❝ *Thus we have looked at the particular terms of these statements in Hebrews, chapter 6 and 10. The important thing to notice is that all these terms together have a definite limit to them. Nowhere are we told that these people were 'born again', that they were regenerate; nowhere are we told that they have been justified; nowhere are we told that they have been sanctified; nowhere are we told that they have been sealed by the Spirit; nowhere are we told that they have been adopted into God's family. I emphasize this for the reason that when references are made to true believers it is always the case that the terms 'justified' and 'sanctified' and so on, are used . . .*

What we are told about these people is not that they are regenerate, not that they are justified, not that they are reconciled to God; but that they have had certain experiences which had brought them into the Church and made them think, and made everyone else think, that they were truly Christian. They had claimed to believe the truth; they had had some remarkable experiences in the realm of the Church together with others, some indeed may even have had some of the miraculous gifts. But all this does not necessarily prove that a man is a Christian, that he is regenerate. **❞**

These people, then, for all their outward appearance, were not true

Christians. Indeed, in Hebrews 6:9 (a key verse for the understanding of this passage), the writer goes on to contrast his readers with them: *'we are confident of better things in your case — things that accompany salvation'.*

Further, we have only to look on to verses 17-20 of Hebrews 6 to see that the doctrine of eternal security is clearly taught in this very chapter. Dr P.E. Hughes writes of these verses:

66 *The personal security of the man whose hope rests on Christ is intended. The metaphor of an anchor in itself effectively portrays the concept of fixity, for the function of an anchor is to provide security in the face of changing tides and rising storms. Human anchors cannot hold man's life secure in the stresses and troubles that assail it; but the anchor of Christian hope is unfailingly sure and steadfast. There is an immense contrast between the former restless and meaningless existence which those who have 'fled for refuge' (verse 18) have left behind them and the stability which, through fixing their confidence in Christ, they now enjoy.* **99**

Jesus Christ our Saviour has already entered heaven, and He has gone ahead to prepare the way for His people (John 14:1-3). Our eternal security depends not upon our actions but upon Christ's. As our High Priest, Jesus prays for us, and this also contributes to the completeness and eternal worth of our salvation (Hebrews 7:25).

What from Christ that soul shall sever,
Bound by everlasting bands?
Once in Him, in Him for ever,
Thus the eternal cov'nant stands:
None shall pluck thee
From the Strength of Israel's hands.
John Kent

25
The Second Coming

Some doctrines are more controversial than others: we have already seen that election and predestination are controversial doctrines, and so too is the teaching about Christ's second coming. On some aspects of this teaching all evangelical Christians are agreed. They all believe that the Lord Jesus will come again to this world, and that His coming will be physical, personal and visible. These things are clearly taught in the Bible (John 14:1-3; Acts 1:11; 1 Thessalonians 4:16-18). But controversy arises over what is meant by the 'thousand years' (or 'millennium') in Revelation 20. On this there are three views:

1. Post-millennialism. Those who hold this view teach that the second coming of Christ will follow the millennium.
2. Pre-millennialism. Christians who believe this teach that Christ's second coming will precede the millennium.
3. A-millennialism or **Non-millennialism.** According to this view, the 'thousand years' of Revelation 20 is to be understood

not literally but figuratively, and there will be no actual millennium.

As we consider the New Testament teaching on the second coming, it will be helpful to ask three basic questions: How? When? Why?

How?

There are some who teach that Christ's second coming is just a spiritual coming, and means His coming to a person at death to take the soul to heaven. That is a lovely thought, but it is not what the New Testament teaches concerning the coming of the Lord. We are told, *'This same Jesus . . . will come back in the same way you have seen him go'* (Acts 1:11). 'This same Jesus' must mean the resurrected Jesus, the physical, bodily Jesus — the One who ate with His disciples (John 21:13-14), the One they saw and touched (Luke 24:39). In the same way as He ascended to heaven — that is, literally, physically and visibly — so He will come back. Or, as Paul puts it, *'the Lord himself will come down from heaven'* (1 Thessalonians 4:16). And when He comes, it will not be

Charles Hodge (1797-1878), professor of theology at Princeton Seminary, USA.

Francis Schaeffer (1912-1984), Christian writer, philosopher and founder of L'Abri Fellowship.

Some of the church's greatest Bible teachers have held different views on the second coming. For instance, Charles Hodge and Jonathan Edwards were post-millennialists; J.C. Ryle and Francis Schaeffer were pre-millennialists; and William Hendriksen and Dr Martyn Lloyd-Jones held to a-millennialism. The fact that such great men could differ on this doctrine should cause the rest of us to be cautious, and to beware of opposing too vigorously fellow-believers who do not share our viewpoint. Perhaps the most helpful comment on this matter is that made by Augustine:

William Hendriksen (1900-1982), author of a well-known series of New Testament commentaries.

" *He who loves the coming of the Lord is not he who affirms that it is far off, nor is it he who says it is near, but rather he who, whether it be far off or near, awaits it with sincere faith, steadfast hope, and fervent love.* "

a secret coming (Matthew 24:30-31).

When?

The first Christians thought that Christ would return in their lifetime, but obviously they were wrong. While the Word of God does give signs of the second coming (Matthew 24), at the same time it says very clearly that no one knows, nor can anyone estimate, when it will be (Matthew 24:36; 1 Thessalonians 5:1-3).

Although the Bible teaches emphatically that the Lord Jesus Christ will come again, it preserves a deliberate air of mystery about the details of His coming. In view of this, we need to beware when someone claims to know all the answers, for in that case he knows more than God has chosen to reveal.

A question often asked is, 'Are we living in the last days?' Scripturally, the answer is yes, because according to Hebrews 1:2 the last days are the days from the birth of Jesus to His second coming. Whether or not these are the last days historically no one can be sure, though many Christians believe that this is so.

Why?

This is by far the most important question. The first coming of Jesus was for salvation, and His second coming will be to complete that salvation. The Christian is a person who is saved now from the guilt and consequence of his sin. His place in heaven is assured; but he is not there yet, and though he is saved from sin, he is still bothered by sin. Salvation will be complete when he sins no more, when he is finally out of the reach and influence of sin, when he is in heaven.

When I stand before the throne,
Dressed in beauty not my own,
When I see Thee as Thou art,
Love Thee with unsinning heart,
Then, Lord, shall I fully know,
Not till then, how much I owe. **"**
Robert Murray M'Cheyne

The view from the summit of Mount Tabor.

Jesus is coming to take His redeemed people to heaven, to the place He has prepared for them (John 14:3). He is coming for all believers of all time — those who have been dead and buried for centuries and those who are alive at the moment (1 Thessalonians 4:16-17). In the light of this great truth, no wonder Paul says, *'Therefore encourage each other with these words'* (verse 18)!

For those who are not Christians the second coming of Christ will be the time of final judgment (1 Peter 3:3-10). Sin will then be dealt with once and for all, and God will bring in *'a new heaven and a new earth, the home of righteousness'* (2 Peter 3:13).

Recommended Books

God's Words: J.I. Packer (Inter-Varsity Press)
Knowing God: J.I. Packer (Hodder & Stoughton)
Redemption Accomplished and Applied: John Murray (Banner of Truth)

A Summary of Christian Doctrine: Louis Berkhof (Banner of Truth)
The Three Are One: Stuart Olyott (Evangelical Press)
What the Scriptures Teach: E.F. Kevan (Evangelical Press)

———General Index———

Page numbers in **bold** show where an entry is the subject of a chapter in the book. Names on maps and charts are not included in the index.

temple, Herod's, 36.
Ten Commandments, 31, 46, 92.
Tertullian, 73.
Tetzel, Johann, 83.
Thanet, Isle of, 72.
Theophilus, 44.
Thessalonica, 47.
Thirty-nine Articles, 96, 119.
Tishri, 39.
Toleration Act (1689), 100.
Toplady, Augustus, 150.
Tozer, A.W., 127, 137, 157.
Trajan (Emperor), 62-63.
translations of the Bible, *see*
   Bible, New Testament, Old
   Testament.
transubstantiation, 76, 78.
Trefecca (Powys), 109.
Trinity, the, **139-141**, 173.
Tuscany, 76.
Tyndale, William, 26, 93, 95:
   martyrdom, 28; translation of
   New Testament, 26-28.

Ulster, 119.
Uniformity, Act of (1662), 100,
   103.
unity, church, 122.

Valencia, Council of (1229), 78.
Valentinian III (Emperor), 72.

vestments, 70.
*View of the State of Religion in
   the Diocese of St. David's,*
   103-104.
Virgin Mary, *see* Mary.
von Staupitz, Johann, 82.
Vulgate, *see* Bible translations:
   Latin.

Waldenses/Waldensians, 78-79.
Waldo, Peter, 78.
Wales, 74, 103-104, 106,
   109-112, 118-119: map of
   South-East, 104. *See also*
   church: Celtic.
Walker, W., 67, 76, 79, 91-92,
   98, 104, 123.
Wartburg (Germany), 85-87.
Watts, Isaac, 107, 146, 150.
Wernos (Powys), 110.
Wesley, Charles, 104, 106-107,
   132, 150, 161.
Wesley, John, 103-104, 106-107,
   109-110.
West, churches of, 26.
Western Wall (Jerusalem), 36.
Westminster: Assembly, 100-101;
   Confession (1647), 99.
Whitefield, George, 103-106,
   109-112, 115, 123.
Wilberforce, William, 117.

William III (King of England),
   100.
Williams, Isaac, 119.
Williams, John, 117.
Williams, William (Pantycelyn),
   110-111.
winnowing, 50.
Wittenberg (Germany), 85.
Word of God, *see* Bible.
World Council of Churches,
   120, 122.
Worms (Germany), 85-86.
worship, 36-37, 70, 93, 107.
Writings, the (division of Jewish
   Bible), 23.
Wycliffe, John, 26, 78-80, 92:
   translation of Bible, 26.

Young, E.J., 18.
Young Men's Christian Associa-
   tion (YMCA), 119.

Zechariah, 35.
Zürich (Switzerland), 88.
Zwingli, Ulrich, 86, 88, 92.

─── Index of Bible References ───

Bible references mentioned in the tables of New Testament miracles
(p.59) and parables (p.57), and also the Bible contents chart (pp.24-25),
have not been indexed.

Old Testament

Genesis, 23, 31, 120.
   1:26, 141; **2:17**, 142, 144; **3**,
   142; **3:1, 4-5**, 142; **3:10**, 143;
   3:22, 141; **4:3-4**, 36; **11:7**, 141;
   17, 31; **22**, 145.
Exodus, 23, 31, 145.
   6:6-7, 162; **12**, 37; **12:13**, 145;
   15:12-13, 162; **33:19**, 173.
Leviticus, 23, 31, 37, 145.
   1:3-4, 36; **16:21-22**, 146; **16**,
   39; **23:26-32**, 39; **23:15-22**, 37;
   23:33-44, 39; **25:25-31**, 162.
Numbers, 23, 31.
Deuteronomy, 23, 31.
   7:7, 172; **16**, 37; **18:5**, 173.
Joshua, 23, 31.
Judges, 23, 31.
Ruth, 23, 31.
   4:2-4, 162.

1 Samuel, 23, 31.
   8:7, 10-20, 32.
2 Samuel, 23, 31.
1 Kings, 23, 31.
   8:16, 173; **8:46**, 168; **11:1-6**,
   32; **12**, 33.
2 Kings, 23, 31.
   18:13-16, 18.
1 Chronicles, 23, 31.
   29:11-12, 127.
2 Chronicles, 23, 31.
   20:6, 127.
Ezra, 23, 31.
   1:2-4, 35.
Nehemiah, 23, 31.
   9:7, 172.
Esther, 23, 31.
Job, 23, 31.
   5:20, 164; **23:13**, 127; **33:4**,
   136.
Psalms, 23, 31, 107.

   19:1, 17; **49:7-8**, 162; **49:15**,
   164; **50:21**, 126; **51**, 156;
   77:14-15, 162; **89:6-8**, 126;
   90:2, 126; **90:10**, 177; **103:19**,
   127; **139:7**, 136.
Proverbs, 23, 31.
Ecclesiastes, 23, 31.
Song of Solomon, 23, 31.
Isaiah, 23, 31.
   6, 141; **6:3,5**, 132; **6:5**, 136;
   40:9-10, 12-26, 28-31, 172;
   40:25, 126; **41:8-9**, 172; **46:5**,
   126; **53:4**, 147; **53:5**, 133; **53:6**,
   146, 160-161.
Jeremiah, 23, 31.
   24:5-7, 35; **25:11**, 33;
   31:33,34, 169; **50:33-34**, 162.
Lamentations, 23, 31.
Ezekiel, 23, 31.
   36:25-27, 169; **36:26-27**, 154.
Daniel, 23, 31.